MANI-
PEDI
STAT

Deb Ebenstein

MANI-
PEDI
STAT

Memoirs of a Jersey Girl
Who Almost Lost Everything

A Vireo Book | Rare Bird Books
Los Angeles, Calif.

A Vireo Book | Rare Bird Books
453 South Spring Street, Suite 531
Los Angeles, CA 90013
rarebirdbooks.com

Set in Myriad
Printed in the United States
Distributed in the US by Publishers Group West

10 9 8 7 6 5 4 3 2 1

Publisher's Cataloging-in-Publication data
Ebenstein, Deb.
    Mani-Pedi stat : memoirs of a Jersey girl who almost lost
everything / by Deb Ebenstein.
    p. cm.
    ISBN 978-1-940207-12-4

1. Ebenstein, Deb—Health. 2. Cancer—Patients—New
Jersey—Biography. 3. Hodgkin's disease—Patients—United
States—Biography. 4. Breast—Cancer—Patients—United
States—Biography. 5. Cancer—Patients—United States—
Family relationships. I. Title.

RC265.6.E24 A3 2014
362.19/6994/0092—dc23

For Andrew, Matthew, and Chloe

Chapter 1

How Big is a Grapefruit?

S UMMER, 1992. I WAS the quintessential Jersey girl entering my junior year of high school—hairspray, lip gloss, dreams of driving around, windows down, in a shiny white Chevy Camaro blasting "Blaze of Glory" on the radio. The whole package. I stood 5'4" with a petite frame and a mass of long, curly brown hair. There were only a few days until the school doors opened. My phone rang. "Hi, you around?" Tina said with a curious giggle. "Yeah, what's up?" "Party at the ball field. You in?" she asked. "Ummm, let me think. Yes." "Great. I'll pick you up in fifteen minutes." "See ya in a few. Love ya." I quickly shoved some essentials into my tote, grabbed a sweatshirt and applied a little extra lip gloss. I puckered my lips in front of the hallway mirror. *Maybe Joey will be at the party*. While Tina leaned on her horn, I rushed to the kitchen to leave a note for my mom. "Went out with friends. Be back later. You'll probably be asleep. I love you."

Ten of us showed up at the field for our last hurrah before commencement. Tina and I hopped up onto the trunk of Eric's car and settled in for what promised to be a fun night. Moments later, a figure in the darkness approached holding something that shimmered in the moonlight. "Yeah! Go Greg!" Joey yelled, once he realized Greg was dragging a keg behind him. *It's a good thing one of these guys looks twenty-one.* The boys spent the next several hours pounding their beers like it was an Olympic sport. I sipped my wine cooler, danced with my girlfriends, and flirted with Joey whenever the opportunity presented itself. It was a typical night in Bergen County, NJ.

Tina dropped me off in front of my house just before 5:00 a.m. I quietly closed the car door, walked up my front porch, and waved goodbye. I grabbed my pink rabbit's foot keychain out of my pocket and slowly turned the key. *Please don't be locked. Please don't be locked.* It clicked. I turned the doorknob and CLANG. *She put the chain on! Shit!* My mother had a liberal parenting style that my brother and I interpreted as: "I trust you. If you do stupid things, the trust is gone. So don't be stupid." I wasn't sure how tonight's behavior would be categorized. I quickly ran down my list of defenses: *I was responsible. I only had three wine coolers in eight hours. I didn't have sex with anyone. I didn't smoke any cigarettes. I didn't get in a car with anyone who was drinking. I didn't commit a crime. I think I'm okay.* What were my options? I could ring the doorbell and she'd be really pissed that I woke her up. I could sit on the porch until seven when she'd be in the kitchen reading *The*

New York Times and having her Sunday morning coffee. I could see if the kitchen window was open and climb through it. *I'm so tired!* I went around back and tried the den door. *Please be open! Oh God. Please, just this once, answer my prayers. Please be unlocked.* The knob turned. *Thank you!* I tiptoed upstairs, crawled under the covers and melted into my mattress where I slept until noon.

I awoke to a beautiful Sunday afternoon. In anticipation of my third year on the varsity volleyball team, I decided to start training before practice officially began. I knew Coach had come to expect a certain skill level from me and I didn't want to disappoint. I strapped on my sneakers and made my way to the high school track. After a mile warm up, I finally reached the bleachers that greeted me every weekend, and began to run up and down the steps with my stopwatch in hand. Up and down, up and down, up and down. Something was wrong. I was out of breath. Not just the regular out of breath, but something different. Something restrictive and strange. I was slow. Too slow. I shrugged it off and powered through. Chalking it up to a late night of partying with my friends, I went home, determined to try again the next day.

The season began and I stood on the very same court where I had stood so many times before. Our first three games were all miserable. My feet too slow, my arms too loose. I knew what I had to do—practice longer and harder. The best thing about sports is that hard work pays off. Practice makes you faster. Weights make you stronger. The recipe had never let me down.

Even as a little girl, I loved skipping, jumping, and running. It simply made me happy. I loved to race my brother down our street and play flag football in the park around the corner. As I got older, I realized organized sports were an opportunity to channel that energy into competition. My parents were athletes, and they constantly encouraged me to challenge myself. Even when they were going through their divorce—a time when they couldn't agree on anything—they still came together to support my brother and me in our athletic endeavors.

My mother told me about growing up on Long Island, shooting hoops in the backyard with her cousins while my grandparents watched with pride. Meanwhile, a thousand miles away in Peoria, Illinois, my father worked as a caddy at the local golf course. When off duty, he collected as many golf balls as he could fit into the pockets of his chinos. The rule of the club was that if you could find it, fish it, or reach it, it was yours. If that meant crawling knee deep into the swampy lake while his fingers crept along the slimy bottom, he did it. The forest teeming with poison ivy?—no problem. Every ball was another swing where he learned to be the golfer he is today.

So even though I'd grown into a boy-obsessed fashion junkie, I was still an athlete. I was doing it all— warming up in practice, running the assigned miles and performing the drills. But my body wasn't responding. In fact, I was regressing. I was missing serves, getting slower on the court, and unable to set the ball for my teammates. I practiced more and more. I stayed late at the gym and worked on my setting. I worked on my spiking and digging. Over and over. But my work didn't translate onto the court. My body just wasn't listening to me.

It didn't make sense. I had grown aware of my strengths and weaknesses, and sports had always been a strength. The whole situation was just, well, odd. By midseason, one of my coaches pulled me aside to ask if everything was okay. "Yes," I told her. "I'm working hard. Even after practice, I'm practicing!"

A few weeks passed and the head coach called me into her office. "Deb, I don't know what's happening, but something is going on. You're just not playing to your potential." I couldn't fight back. I couldn't argue. She was right. I was not pulling my weight on the court. She dropped me from the starting lineup. I was devastated. I sat on the bench across from the bleachers filled with friends and family and listened to the echo of the ball bouncing off my teammates' arms. I wore the uniform, but I might as well have been wearing a T-shirt that said "FAILURE" in thick red permanent marker. I was humiliated. I was more than humiliated. I was downright pissed. *What the hell is going on?* Game after game, I sat beside the court and tried to suppress my feelings of disappointment so they didn't spill all over the gym floor.

December finally came and the season ended. After our last game, I ripped my uniform from my exhausted body and returned it to the sports utility room for hibernation until next season. The outfit that once made me feel strong and empowered strangely morphed into a symbol of my shortcomings. I was glad to put the season behind me. I exhaled. *It's over.* No more expectations. No more embarrassment and disappointment. I'd just pretend none of this ever happened.

I took some time off from sports. I continued to feel tired and worn out but didn't think much of my winter blues. Who doesn't want to take a nap in the middle of a snowy day? Little oddities showed themselves, but I could have never imagined what I was in for. Then, in March, my body stopped whispering and started to scream.

One night, I spiked a fever. I took Tylenol, but the fever persisted. Several days passed. My mom took me to the pediatrician, who found that the glands below my jaw line were extremely swollen. *Shit! Do I have mono?* Although I hadn't been kissing any boys lately—I'd been too tired, sloth-like in my fatigue—it was entirely possible I'd contracted the virus from all the lip gloss my girlfriends shared. Given my age and symptoms, mononucleosis was the initial hypothesis. During those first few fever-filled days and nights I spent in bed, my friends left obnoxious yet funny messages on my answering machine. "Hey Deb! Heard Billy Robertson got mono last week, too. And I thought you hated him. You tramp!" My brother, a sophomore in college, called with his own jabs. A few days later, the initial test came back negative for mono. *Thank God. Mono is horrible.* But then my pediatrician decided to re-run the labs, expecting that the first test was a false negative. Three negative mono tests and four weeks of fever later, my body stopped screaming and proceeded into full-blown hysteria. Night after night, sweat seeped through my pajamas, blanket, sheets, and towel. Sometimes it happened twice a night. My mother and I followed the lead of the pediatric team that I had seen all my life and waited patiently. Finally, acknowledging that they were out of their league, they sent me to the local hospital for further testing.

I was anxious. A hospital visit is considerably more daunting than a small pediatric office. But at that point, I simply needed relief. I didn't care where I was sent as long as someone could fix me. I was escorted into the radiology department. *What's radiology?* A technician performed an X-ray of my chest. "Lift your arms." "Good, turn right. Lift them again." "Good." Shortly thereafter, a nameless doctor walked into the waiting room and informed my mother that there was a "shadow" in my chest and that we would need to go to a hospital better equipped to handle this kind of issue. My antenna shot up. *This kind of issue? What does that mean? This must be a really crappy hospital if they can't even a handle a fever. I need antibiotics. Or something.*

Anything. I feel awful. Although I keenly watched my mother's eyes dilate and her posture tighten, I wasn't processing any of it.

The local hospital scheduled an appointment for me at a high tech medical center for 9:00 a.m. the next day. We went home, ate dinner and I collapsed into bed. I wasn't scared. I just wanted to feel better. The following morning I ate breakfast, showered, and flipped on the TV. My mother was in the kitchen cleaning the stove. It was 8:30, 8:45, 9:15 and we were both wandering around the house. Neither of us looked at the clock. There was something in the air that morning. Denial? Fear? At 9:30 a.m. the phone rang. "Yes, of course, we're coming," my mother swiftly said before clicking the phone back into place. More denial? More fear? There was just one more dish my mother needed to clean. There was just one more show I needed to watch. At 11:30 a.m. the phone rang again. This time I heard a woman's voice barreling through the receiver. "Where are you?" she demanded. I caught my mother's eye. We stared at each other. She wasn't actively expressing her anxiety. She was trying to protect me. I followed her lead and packed my bag. Finally we got into the car.

I was trained to believe that doctors fix our medical problems. Have a cavity? Get it filled. Have a headache? Take an aspirin. Sprain an ankle? Ice packs. There's always an answer. And for some annoying reason, no one had figured out my answer yet. I guess that's because they weren't asking the right questions. Neither was I. "When am I going to get better?" I wondered, rather than "Am I ever going to get better?" My mother's thoughts, however, reflected her experience. She wasn't a teenager, full of priceless naïveté and optimism.

Strangely enough, it was actually energizing for me to leave my bedroom and enter this new facility, a place that might finally give me the relief I'd been looking for. I was focused on one thing: tomorrow. I wanted to get back to school, slide on the eggplant colored jeans and matching plaid bodysuit that had been hanging over my desk chair for weeks, and re-enter my world of adolescent drama and excitement. I almost forgot that there was a huge party that upcoming weekend. I needed to get better so that I could get Danny Digliano to notice me. I really thought I'd be in and out of the hospital in a few days.

We arrived at the medical center at noon, carrying the same beige-piped hunter green duffle that I usually brought to slumber parties. But this time, instead of packing Oreos and teen magazines instructing me on the fine art of homemade avocado-mayo facials, my bag held two pairs of pajamas, a toothbrush, toothpaste, and my SAT prep materials. The automatic doors opened with a swoosh of air. The building was massive—it looked more like a conference center than a medical facility. Everywhere I turned there were adults in suits and ties and white coats. Okay, I'll admit it…I was a little intimidated. Not by anyone's status or age, but by the sheer mechanism. It felt like we had walked into a machine with countless moving parts and the farther inside we ventured, the more we became part of the matrix. I was so focused on returning to my daily life—a feeling still so palpable, so appropriately narcissistic— that I was spared the fear this initiation should have incited.

I smiled as I looked around. Everything was color-coded, like someone with major obsessive-compulsive issues had taken a hit of acid and gone berserk on the place. The red building was to the right, the yellow building to the left, the green elevator went to the eighth floor, where you'd make a left at the orange sign and then a right at the purple staircase and you'd get to the land of Oz. *Where's the wizard?*

I followed my mother towards the information desk. We gave the woman behind the counter our names and informed her that we were scheduled to see Dr. D. She looked up at my mother, and then she looked at me. I'd never seen this look before. She was staring at me with wide eyes, but she didn't smile. It was like she knew who I was but we had never met. She instructed us to use the last bank of elevators on the left and then walk through the glass corridor. I shrugged. *She is weird.* We followed her directions and arrived at a set of huge glass doors with a sign that read, "Authorized Personnel Only." *Well, that's definitely not us.* But sure enough, my mom pressed the large silver button on the side of the wall. Like the gates of heaven, the glass doors swung open. *What makes us "Authorized"?* I felt sort of special, like I was just given a secret hall pass. I had no idea what was about to happen.

We made a right turn down the Clorox-white hallway, and I looked up to see a sign on the wall with an arrow that said "Pediatric Hematology & Oncology." There was no fainting, no shock, nothing at all. My youth was the ultimate shield. I knew I was on a pediatric floor because there were kids walking through the halls. I also realized it was indeed a cancer floor because most of the kids were bald. *Oh man. They stuck me on this floor. Oh well. The broken arm or tonsillectomy floor must have been booked. Damn—I bet they had good ice cream on that floor.* It was inconceivable to believe anything else.

A nurse greeted us at the end of the hallway and brought me into a room. There was a paper sign taped to the door that had my first initial and last name in large black letters. *Cool.* The room had a bed, television, dresser, and private bathroom. *Awesome—this is more privacy than I get at home.* The doctors and nurses all introduced themselves and repeated the phrase used at the previous hospital. They said, "Deb, we see a shadow in your chest X-ray." *Okay. Is that supposed to mean something to me?* They continued to speak to me with kid gloves. "You know what floor you are on, right? This is the pediatric oncology floor." I responded, "Yes." *I'm not an idiot; I can read the sign.* Denial had jumped into my body and was swinging away with its weaponry. A nurse asked me to undress and change into the hospital gown someone had thoughtfully placed on the bed. I obliged and then waited. *It is freezing like the tundra, and they want me to wear this piece of cloth?* The coolness factor quickly diminished.

I unzipped my bag and took out the same cozy gray high-school volleyball sweatshirt that I wore to the field party. I grabbed the sleeves and inhaled its scent. Had I not washed it since that night? It smelled like cut grass and debauchery. *Oh well.* I threw it over the gown and immediately felt more like myself. Despite the horrific volleyball season, my team colors still brought me feelings of confidence and power. As I flipped through some magazines, a cheery nurse, holding a clipboard covered with stickers of bears jumping over rainbows, began asking questions. Lots of questions. "Do you know why you are here?" "Yes, I have a questionable shadow in my chest and I feel like crap." I responded. "Do you know what floor this is?" I cringed. *Do they think I'm slow or something? I can read. I can see the other kids. So, duh...I'm obviously aware I'm on the oncology floor!* Their bizarre repetitive questioning was really starting to annoy me. The other floors must be fully booked, I thought, like I was staying at the Ritz Carlton in Buenos Aires. I had no idea they had already concluded that I was about to join this club of bald kids walking down the hallways attached to IV poles. "Yes, of course," I replied in annoyance. She looked down at her list and began the lengthy process of intake. What's your full name? What school do you attend? Have you ever been hospitalized? Have you ever had surgery? She asked about my previous health, diet, exercise, family history of every illness on the planet, legal drugs, illegal drugs, alcohol consumption (or not), sexual activity (or not), current symptoms, and length of symptoms. I answered most of the questions quickly and easily, and looked at my mother for clarification when we arrived at something I didn't know. It was the truth when I said, "Nope, no drugs. Never." I lied when I said, "Nope, no alcohol. Never." I couldn't imagine a few Bartles & Jaymes wine coolers mattered much at this point. At the end of the interview the nurse simply nodded and then ran down the list of tests I was about to endure.

Another woman entered my room smiling sheepishly. From the expression on her face I thought she was about to offer me a sparkling beverage. This was not the case. Instead, she took my arm, daubed it with rubbing alcohol, and inserted my very first IV. She packed up all her equipment, threw the garbage into the fire engine red hazardous materials box and said, "Hang in there." She gave me a peculiar smile and left the room. I felt like I did downstairs at the Information Desk. I realized that all the bizarre looks, questions, and funny little feelings inside my gut were not coincidental. They were leading somewhere. Somewhere big.

The day continued full speed ahead. I was a little squeamish and totally exhausted. Is this what they mean when they say, "Put through the ringer?" An aid walked in a few hours later with a wheelchair. "What's this about?" I asked. She said, "I'm here to escort you to your scan." I snarkily responded, "I think you have the wrong room, ma'am." *How dare this woman come into my room and imply that I need a wheelchair. Can't she see that I'm fully capable of walking? I'm an athlete. I'm wearing my varsity letters for goodness sake.* She then confirmed my name and room number. It was my name, my room number. Deflation. Although I informed her I could easily walk, it was hospital policy to be driven to each test regardless of mobility. I knew this was a safety concern, but with each command my autonomy slipped further away. I had moved into a new world, with its own set of laws. The coolness factor was gone. In case I hadn't taken the hint that I was now a patient in a world where I had minimal control, the nurse finished me off: "Honey, please take off your sweatshirt. You must be in your gown for the exam. If you're cold I can get you a blanket from the utility room." *I hate this place!*

After several elevator rides through various wings of the hospital, we reached our destination and the first test began. I was placed lying down, face up, on a cold silver plank. My aid left the room. A moment later, the technician walked in. His name was Dean. He was in his twenties and he was kind of cute. I was embarrassed that I didn't have clothes on. I was wearing the hideous hospital gown. *How am I supposed to flirt with this guy wearing this piece of cloth and an IV pole?* My bubble abruptly burst when he explained what was going to happen. *This isn't sexy. Oh, right, I'm a patient. I'm supposed to be listening and then doing something right now. Play along, Deb, play along.*

"Have you ever had a CAT scan before?" he asked.

"Nope, never," I replied, smiling coyly.

"Well, I'm going to connect your IV to a special dye that lets me see certain things in your body. The dye can have some affects so it's really important that you tell me if you are feeling anything. Okay?"

"No problem," I replied, still smiling.

Dean covered me with another blanket (since it was so damn cold in there) and said, "Okay, here we go." The icy dye pulsed through the needle into my arm and within seconds I began to feel some weird stuff.

"Dean, I feel like I have pennies in my mouth."

"Yes, Deb, that's normal. Don't worry, it will go away."

I can handle this. This is no big deal. Then, something weird started to happen. I felt warm inside. Like a heater was turned on inside my body. It didn't hurt. It actually felt nice considering I was so freakin' cold. But where did I feel warm you ask? DOWN THERE! There was no way I was telling this guy about the sensation I was having. *What's happening? Is this normal?* In case this side effect was the precursor to a seizure or something, I mustered up the courage to say, "Ummm, Dean. I feel mildly warm. Is that normal?"

"Oh, yeah, definitely," he said. He spared me the utter embarrassment of spelling out the details and just validated that I wasn't a total freak.

Dean walked into a separate room behind my head. He clicked on a PA system and said, "Okay, I'm going to tell you to hold your breath for five seconds. I'll let you know when you can breathe." My heart raced. *I'm scared.* The machine turned on. It sounded like a loud and ancient computer booting up. I heard the click of the PA and then his voice: "Hold your breath, five, four, three, two, one. Okay. Breathe. Hold your breath. Five, four, three, two, one. Okay, breathe." *Why does Dean keep leaving the room? Why does he need to be behind a glass door?* I could only assume something dangerous was inside my end of the room. So why was I still lying there?

After the CAT scan was over, a different tech escorted me back to my room where the team was waiting for me. Dr. D began to speak. "I'm going to be performing a biopsy on you tomorrow. You feel those swollen glands on your neck? I'm going to remove a piece of one so we can test it and figure out what's going on. Is that okay with you?" *Is this okay with me? Ummm...I'm going to have surgery—General anesthesia, scalpels, a breathing tube. Ummm...no!*

"You need to do this, right?" I asked.

"Yes, to make you better. We do."

"Okay, then do it." It was a two-day marathon of pricks, prods, questions, scans, and scalpels. All while wearing the hideous off-white gown (originally pure white, I suspect) with the phrase "Property of Hospital X" stamped all over and my butt sticking out the back.

As I was recovering in my room from the biopsy surgery, and thinking about the scar that would forever mark my neck, the door opened. Dr. D, along with two nurses and my mother, walked in, single file, and surrounded my hospital bed. They had my test results.

The next twenty minutes would be forever burned into my brain. It was April 29, 1993. I was sixteen years old. Three days before I was supposed to take the SAT. I felt like I was hovering over my body watching everything from above. I wanted to shout, "This can't be happening. Are they speaking English? Slow down. I'm not even present yet!" One day I was a high school student, playing sports and thinking about college. Then, out of nowhere, eight not-so-simple words changed my life. Dr. D calmly stated, "You have cancer, Deb. It's called Hodgkin's Disease." Like an avalanche, everything turned white. The intensity consumed me. Was I frozen? Was I burning? I was searching for a life vest but had no idea where to look. In an instant, everything started to spin—my life, body, family, friends, expectations, and future were all tossed into a rocket ship and shot into space. *Where the fuck am I?* A war was beginning.

"Deb," my doctor said. "Deb, did you hear me?"

My hovering self said, "Yeah, buddy, I heard you. I'm just trying to not faint and die of shock." I mentally returned to the room, stiffened my posture, and sat up in the hospital bed.

My mother stood beside the team of white coats. Her eyes were watery, and there was no mistaking her fear. *Mommy never gets scared.* Although petite, my mother is a warrior. She effortlessly combines strength with grace. She reserves her softness for those she holds dear, and I have always felt privileged to be her daughter—to have such a role model. She takes crap from no one. My brother's friends used to invite him over to play catch. One day he said, "Let's go to my house. It's so much closer." His friends declined. "Your mother scares the shit out of us." She isn't actually scary, but she's very intimidating—her strength and determination are impossible to miss.

So in that moment, when our world was collapsing around us, my mother's force was ever so present. She stood in front of me, eyes locked on mine, wishing she could stare off the fatal thoughts permeating the room.

I looked slightly to my left, baffled by the array of faces focused singularly on me, waiting for the ticking time bomb to explode. Silence. I felt like a spectacle. Dr. D continued to sternly inform me that the cancer had spread to many regions of my body including my neck, chest, and pelvis. *This isn't good.* Immediate administration of chemotherapy was necessary and he was not sugar-coating the issue. Anger welled up inside of me. Dr. D may as well have been the Devil incarnate. Without thought, I ordered everyone out. I just started screaming. No thought, just reaction. "Get out! Get out of my room!" I looked around: the gray plastic water pitcher, the bed pan sitting idle on the night stand, the flickering halogen lights, the IV protruding from my hand, the oxygen tank attached to the wall. *No, no, no, no, no, no, no,* no*!* With all my might, I wanted to throw something heavy and glass against the cement block wall and make it shatter into a million pieces. I wanted to scream and punch and defend and protest. I felt like breathing fire and incinerating everything around me. I sat with my head between my legs, swaying back and forth with a vengeance, trying to figure out how this could happen. *No one asked my permission for any of this. Who is responsible for this outrageous diagnosis?* Like I was at Gap asking to speak to a manager to complain about a mispriced sweater—I was frantically searching for someone to right this wrong. I screamed, cried, punched the wall, and thought I was going to die—way before the cancer killed me—of true rage. After an hour, I had nothing left. I collapsed with the ripped pillow over my head. Then, suddenly, the door opened. *Who in their right mind is coming back in here? I am about to kick someone's ass.*

I had never seen this guy before. First off, he was smiling. The other guys didn't smile. His face was round and friendly with a full head of curly black hair. He walked with confidence. Almost annoyingly so. He was wearing a suit and tie sans the white coat. *One point for Mr. X: He's not a doctor.*

"I'm Dr. W," he said calmly. *Sneaky bastard.*

"Why aren't you wearing a white coat?" I asked.

"Well, I'm the oncology psychologist." There was that word again. *Oncology.* What word is worse to a sixteen-year-old—*Oncology* or *Psychologist? So they think I have cancer, and I'm crazy.*

His next stab at engaging me was, "So, you just got diagnosed, huh?" *Is this guy for real?* I stared at him in silence. "I hear you kicked everyone out," he said. Then, I got it. *They have no idea what to do with me and brought you down here to handle it.* I said nothing. We sat like that, or rather I sat and he stood, in silence, until he asked, "Do you like pie?" *Do I like pie? What's this guy's deal?* I just wanted to be left alone. I wanted to cry and scream without anybody pestering me. I had a thick shell of anger coating the gut wrenching, unimaginable fear of facing my mortality that I needed to attend to, and this guy was talking about pie. *Dude, go up to your fancy shmancy office, pull those degrees off your wall and throw them in the garbage.*

"No, I don't eat pie," I said.

"Hmm. Maybe later," he continued. He opened his mouth and words spilled out. I went into a sort of trance, watching his mouth move without hearing any words. Minutes passed. Maybe ten. Maybe fifty. His voice was soothing, so I let his tone act as a musical background. It wasn't U2, but it was something other than perpetual beeps from various monitors in the hallway.

All of a sudden, I snapped back as he muttered, "There's some apple pie in the cafeteria. It's really good. I think you'll like it. Let me get some." I was exhausted. Too confused to respond. He wore me down. Making himself at home, he picked up the phone sitting on the rolling cart used for breakfast, lunch, and dinner. "Hi, this is Dr. W. Could I have some apple pie delivered to Room 246 please? Thank you." *What just happened? Should I be looking for hidden cameras in the walls? Is this some sort of joke?* I thought shrinks were supposed to be on the money, but this guy was acting like I just told him I was going to get a wart removed. He continued to talk as I floated in and out of consciousness. The door opened again and a hospital aid delivered a cafeteria tray with a piece of apple pie on it. She positioned the cart in front of me and left the room. Dr. W said, "Try it." There was so much anguish pulsing through my veins that it almost transformed into laughter. But no. I wouldn't give him that. "I'm not hungry," I replied coldly.

"Okay, maybe later then," he responded.

I just wanted to be left alone but he wouldn't leave!

"So, you are taking the SATs?" he asked.

For a second I thought he might be clairvoyant, but then I noticed my prep book sitting on my bedside table next to the emergency oxygen tank. At this point I'd become so anxious that if I actually allowed myself to feel all the fear, pressure, expectation, and seriousness of the situation, I would not only need the oxygen tank, but a crash cart as well. Dr. W's candor disarmed me and I realized he wasn't going to leave. *Okay, whatever Deb. Just talk to this guy.* I flipped through the SAT booklet. "I've been studying and I'm ready to take the exam. It's 9:00 a.m. this Saturday in my high school cafeteria. I'm assuming I can't go."

Dr. W's brilliant approach, as he would love for it to be called, accessed the part of me that had been asked to check herself at the door. I was still a regular

teenager seeking autonomy and respect. Dr. W knew
that a calm or rational Deb just wasn't available at the
moment. My life was crashing down around me. After
talking for a while he said, "I know this really sucks."
It does! It was dark and horrible and so damn scary.
There was nothing he could have said or done in those
moments to ease my pain. And I don't believe that was
his mission. His goal was to stay in my room, treat me
like a sixteen-year-old girl wishing she was wearing her
own perfectly coordinated outfit, and withstand my
rage. He understood that only then would I be able to
come back to earth and start talking. I didn't eat the pie,
but I did press the little red button on the side of my bed
and tell the nurse I was ready to see everyone.

The door opened. My mother was the first to step
back inside, and then the doctors, nurses, and social
worker followed. Dr. D began to speak. This was not a
dream. It was in fact very real. My heart was racing and
I began to sweat.

I had obviously heard about various forms of
cancer—breast, bone, and liver—but never Hodgkin's
Disease. *What is this thing inside me? It doesn't even
sound like cancer.* When I heard cancer, I thought death.
It was almost easier that Hodgkin's didn't have cancer in
its name. I learned about my lymph system and what it
meant when cancer snuck its way inside. Since the lymph
system travels throughout your body, it unfortunately
can serve as an express train for cancerous cells. The
doctor explained that cancerous cells are abnormal

cells that take over the healthy ones. When they pool together, they form tumors. My largest tumor was in my chest and was approximately the size of a grapefruit. *A grapefruit? How is it possible that I don't see something the size of grapefruit sticking out of my chest?* Dr. D then explained "staging." Within a particular diagnosis, there are stages, degrees of severity. Within Hodgkins, there are seven stages. From minor to major, they are as follows: stage 1A, 1B, 2A, 2B, 3A, 3B, and 4. I was staged at 3B because of the size of my tumor. When I received this bit of news, everything went black. Whether it was in the movies or in reality, most of the people I knew died from this aggressive disease. Was death my fate as well? Only time would tell. But before I went completely boneless, the team quickly followed this shocking news with their feelings of confidence in the treatment and prognosis. The statistics were in my favor, and they were hopeful that I could win this battle. There was no way to fix the fight, but I was going to do everything asked of me to make sure I gave my body the best chance for survival. I began to listen to my new coaches.

Dr. D laid out the game plan. "You're going to receive eight rounds of chemotherapy. The medications will be administered on an outpatient basis downstairs at the clinic. Some of the chemo is in pill form, but most of the treatments will be intravenous drugs. Following the completion of chemo, you'll undergo three months of radiation targeting your chest, abdomen, and pelvic areas. Before any of this begins, we need to insert a catheter into your chest. It will make everything easier and you won't need to get an IV every time you have a treatment. Your catheter can be accessed instead."

Oh, that's it? Approximately nine months of chemotherapy followed by three months of radiation. *I can do this. No I can't. Yes, I can. FUCK!*

Once I saw an opening where I could interject, I turned blankly to the team, almost breathless, and asked, "Okay. So when is my treatment going to begin?" *I can't believe I just used the word "treatment." Oh my God—deep breath.*

Dr. D calmly stated, "Tonight, Deb."

"Tonight?" I exclaimed. My developmental age was never more apparent. I wasn't seven, twenty-five, thirty-eight, or sixty-two—I was sixteen. I was just diagnosed with a life threatening illness. Now the doctor was telling me that the medicine that was going to make me sick as a dog, gain weight, and put my life on hold was starting *tonight*? I looked at my mother who appeared to be hanging on by a thread. "But Mommy, that doesn't work. I have the SATs on Saturday." I knew it was a long shot. Perhaps in some magical parallel universe, the white coats surrounding my hospital bed would say, "Oh, of course. We understand. When would you like to start? If at all, actually." Instead, they looked up at me like I was on some sort of hallucinogenic. My mother, on the other hand, understood what was important in my former reality. "Well, honey, we'll just have to reschedule." I was grasping at anything that would bring me back to my previous world. I grabbed my sweatshirt and buried my head inside it. I cried some more. I was an emotional ping-pong ball bouncing off feelings of betrayal, violation, perplexity, fear, and utter speechlessness. My mind repeated the words over and over in my head: *I have cancer. I have cancer. I have cancer. Okay, I have this disease. Say it again? Wait just a minute; wasn't I at the mall a few weeks ago with my friends trying on designer dresses? Cancer patients don't do that. Didn't I just plan the great escape out of my mother's house? Cancer patients don't do that.* The room was silent. *Please, please, please let this be a dream.* But I opened my eyes and they were still staring at me. I knew that I must consent. Consent—a word with an entirely new meaning. Did I have to do it? No. Must I to possibly survive? Yes. Just when I thought it couldn't get any worse, I remembered the kids in the hallway. Oh shit. I grabbed my brown locks with both hands and exclaimed, "My hair!" *Please don't let me lose my hair; please don't let me lose my hair!*

Although the era of the eighties hair band had just ended, the quintessential Jersey girl was still deeply embedded within me, and I needed my volume, curl, and daily dose of hairspray. A huge part of my identity was wrapped up in my shiny, brown, curly locks. I lived in a world where every teen magazine and Pantene commercial showcased beautiful models as they tossed their waves from side to side. It would've been quite a feat to grow up not believing that hair was an integral part of beauty. Beauty brought smiles from strangers on the street and a plethora of friends by your side. Compliments feel good. How would people react to me bald? Would they pity me? Would they still want to be my friend? Would I lose my eyebrows? My eyelashes? Although the medical team moved onto more pressing subjects, I was stuck—and I mean stuck—on the hair issue. Who cares about nausea when you have to go to your prom bald?! I just wanted to look like me, even though it was beginning to sound like I'd never be the same again. The doctor confirmed that my hair would start falling out in approximately two weeks. I was shaking from head to toe.

How is this happening? Where am I? I felt like Alice in Wonderland, falling down the rabbit hole and spinning into an abyss of craziness. I had landed at the bottom of the well and now, staring back at me, was some girl stripped of her clothes, hair, and body. I had no structure to hold my identity. No vessel that felt familiar. I knew things were about to be different. Forever.

The seventh day of my medical marathon included the biopsy surgery, catheter insertion surgery, first round of chemotherapy treatment, and what felt like dozens of scans, tests, and blood draws. Finally, the nurse walked in and said, "You're going home." At first, I exhaled with relief. But then she followed it up with this: "We'll see you tomorrow."

My mother and I went home, unpacked, washed the hospital smell out of our clothes, and curled up beside the television. The next morning I woke up in her bed and she was already in the shower. For a few seconds I thought the previous day's activities were all part of a dream, but then my heart sank. It truly ached. I had heard of heartache before, usually in the midst of a Lionel Richie love song, but I had no idea that when things get seriously heavy, the heart actually does hurt.

Wearing my own pink and yellow pajamas instead of that horrible hospital gown, I reached down my nightshirt and brushed my hand over my chest. I felt the bandage where the catheter lay beneath. *Oh boy. Here come the tears again.* And the sobbing began. It was uncontrollable. I was crying for so many reasons I couldn't even begin to separate or understand them. As the shower turned off and my mother opened the bathroom door, I jumped across the hallway to my bedroom and wiped my eyes. I pulled myself together and reemerged a few minutes later. We made a list of the dozens of prescriptions that had to be filled and errands that needed to be run before we began our new life. My mother picked up the phone and called my father. Since the divorce, they hadn't spoken more than a few words, but this was an extraordinary circumstance. There was no room for rage or revenge—their daughter was sick.

I'm not sure if it was conscious or not, but I set a goal for myself. I was going to be the same person that I'd been a few days ago. The girl before the diagnosis. I had no idea that my objective was so much more complicated than the rest of the bullet points on our to-do list.

Like most teenagers, I tried to separate myself from my parents. Sometimes I was rebellious, but mostly I just craved independence. But no matter what age, my mom and I have always enjoyed shining light on dark days with a visit to the shops to pick up a trinket. We'd buy a silver and turquoise bracelet cuff that we could share, or a new jean jacket that Mom refused to let me bleach or rip because it was brand new. Maybe even a trip to the local bakeshop for a piece of fresh seven-layer cake with two forks. We both knew that our excursions wouldn't solve our problems, but even if the pleasure lasted only a moment, it was worth it because it made us smile and we did it together. After days of utter chaos, in and out of hospitals, a ridiculous cancer diagnosis and few hours of sleep, we went shopping. How could I be thinking about fashion at a time like this? Easily—really easily. I bought a new pair of cutoff jean shorts with patchwork sewn along the bottom and a matching black shirt with spaghetti straps. To top it off, we sauntered over to the shoe department. I slipped on a pair of black suede clogs that had the highest wedge heels I had ever been allowed to wear. Given my nonexistent social calendar for the next several months, they weren't the most practical pair of shoes, but we threw caution to the wind. I knew that when I walked through the doors of my high school the following day, every single person in the building would be talking about me. At the very least, I would feel cute in my perfectly assembled new look. As a teenage girl, my notion of what was important in life was limited to giggling with friends and crying endlessly over a boy that didn't like me back. That life may have been over, but it was still the only life I knew.

With my mother by my side, I opened the doors to my high school, reveling in the vibrating clickity-clack of my new clogs as my footsteps echoed down the front hall. High heels always make a girl feel powerful and sexy—even a girl who's walking cancer. My mother entered the principal's office to discuss the logistics of my schedule, given the flexibility I would need in the coming months. I was hell-bent on completing my junior and senior years as originally planned. I didn't care if I had to cram for exams during my treatments with an IV bag dangling from my arm. I just wanted to graduate with my class.

As my mother met with the principal, I headed upstairs to the school newspaper office to take my senior photo for the following year's yearbook. It was the last day to take senior pictures, and if I didn't take it now, there would be a blank box above my name for the rest of time, and I sure as hell wasn't going to let that happen. It was seven days after my diagnosis. I looked the same; long, dark, curly hair, pink complexion, killer outfit. I entered the room at the end of hall. The photographer was waiting for me. I was the last picture. He looked up and said, "Oh, you're here. Great. I was just about to leave. Let's get this going." He politely asked me to wrap the black cape over my shirt, grab a rose from the table and place it across my chest. I started to sweat. This wasn't the way this moment was meant to go down. Senior picture was supposed to be epic. It should represent accomplishment and joy. But all I felt was fear, anger, and more fear. This couldn't really be happening, could it? Although I still looked like me before cancer—and maybe that's how everyone would remember me when they opened our yearbook decades later—I had already changed. I turned to the light. The photographer clicked his camera and took a picture of a girl. Not the girl who walked these halls for the past three years. I'd become somebody I didn't yet understand. My smile, my laugh, and my tears would forever be so much more complicated than the person in that yearbook picture.

I pulled myself together and headed downstairs to meet my mother. As I walked down the hall, I heard squeaky, excited voices coming my way. My crew of girlfriends ran towards me. I saw their faces and smiled for the first time in weeks. "Awesome outfit!" they shrieked. "Your legs look killer in those shorts." *Thank God some things haven't changed.*

Chapter 2

Bear

WHEN I WAS TEN years old, a typical goodnight routine included picking out a pair of rhinestone-studded pajamas, brushing my teeth with a Hello Kitty timer to make sure I completed a lengthy dental regimen, and sincerely saying good night to each of the twenty-five stuffed animals aligned on my bed. To name a few, there was Toto the puppy dog, Sandy the kitten, Bongo the monkey, Pegasus the unicorn, Smurfette, Snuggle, and Caroline. In collection, they were my security blanket. Individually, each possessed its own personality, inhibited or exuberant, but the common thread that joined them was their loyalty. We were all in it together.

It had been one month since my diagnosis and I was already returning to the pharmacy to collect refills on various prescriptions. I had roamed the aisles of this Rite Aid for so many years, often pondering which magazine to buy or—if I was feeling adventurous enough—whether to buy plastic tampons instead of cardboard. This time was different. While I waited for the pharmacist to assemble my package of poison, I found myself sauntering down the seven-year-old girl aisle. The shelves were filled with shrinky dinks, Play-Doh, and stuffed animals. There was nothing sad about this space, just happy memories from a simpler time. Instinctively, I reached over and picked up a large, dark brown stuffed bear with black eyes and white paws. I had forgotten how soft these furry creatures are when you first buy them, before years of abuse and dozens of washing machine cycles strip their fuzziness. I heard someone call out my name and walked back to the pharmacy. I reached for my wallet and the cashier politely asked, "Are you getting the bear, too?" I smiled, initially thinking, *Whoops...of course not.* But then I stopped and thought, *Why the hell not?* The bear made me smile, and life, at that moment, needed to be filled with as much happy as possible. I looked up at the cashier and responded with glee: "Yes, and the bear, too." He was a soft, snuggly, warm companion that ended up lying by my bedside as my eyes filled with tears, my heart with sorrow, and my body with pain. There were days when I couldn't muster the physical strength to shower or brush my teeth. He, Teddy, was always there to comfort me. He absorbed my tears and never judged me when I smelled like a garbage can. You can't really be a burden to a stuffed animal.

Advice flowed in from all ends of the universe. What foods would make me feel better, what holistic remedies might ease the nausea, what smells stimulate serenity, what movies might distract me—everything and anything was pouring in. Most of the information barreling through the door came from my mother's friends who had experienced cancer themselves or knew someone else who did. My friends, of course, were absolutely clueless and continued to talk about exams, boys, and tan lines. *Thank God!* There was a general consensus from my mother's crew that my hair was going to eventually fall out and that I needed to prepare for the inevitable. And so began the wig discussions. *Yuck.* My mother and I were following each other blindly into this new world, and it seemed logical to buy a wig in preparation for what promised to be a physical and psychological nightmare.

So, off we went to the I-have-cancer-so-I-need-a-wig store. We were met by every kind of hairdo imaginable. The wigs were blonde, brunette, black, straight, wavy, curly, short, long, thin, thick, and each was on a mannequin hanging off the wall. *Can you say creepy?* The saleswoman greeted us at the door and gave me the "How are you doing, honey?" face. She wore way too much make-up and had long pointy nails painted with zebra stripes. Her dagger-like fingers proceeded to "fit" my head for twenty minutes. Then she broke out the sample wigs. It was like a horror film! They were itchy and uncomfortable with hard plastic liners that were supposed to form to my scalp. "Honey, I know it feels weird now but once your hair is gone, it will feel much better." *This will never feel better. This isn't my hair. It doesn't feel like my hair, it doesn't smell like my hair, it doesn't look like my hair!* I hated every second of the process, but I tried to believe what everyone around me was saying: "You're going to love it. No one will ever know the difference." *Who isn't going to know the difference? A monkey?* I might not have been around the cancer block, but I knew that no matter what anyone said, this wig was obviously for me and no one else. It was clearly not my hair. I wouldn't be fooling anyone, but I guess it would help me avoid the everyday stares of strangers checking out the girl with the glistening bald head. *Give it a chance, Deb. Grin and bear it.* A few days later, my wig arrived, and I hated it. I placed it on my desk chair, still in the plastic bag.

I was four weeks into chemo and I woke up every morning prepared to find clumps of hair on my pillow. The same pillow that covered the tooth fairy's prized notes praising me for taking the loss of my tooth like a champ. That didn't seem so long ago. Oh, how I needed a fairy with magic sparkly dust. But the clump phase never came. Instead, hairs slowly fell out and gathered on my bed, on the carpet, and in the drain after my morning shower. It was insufferable. Sometimes I'd skip the shower just so I didn't have to deal with what I would find. Gross, I know.

It was Saturday night. My friends were at the movies. My mom was downstairs with a girlfriend having coffee and cake. I sat on my bed with a razor in one hand and scissors in the other. The suspense of losing my hair was killing me. It was like walking around for days and weeks waiting to be punched in the face. After years of pining for the straight, frizz-less hair of some of my peers, I'd never been so appreciative of my endless curls and an inability to wear bangs. The weight of its texture, color, length, and shine wouldn't matter if it wasn't there at all. The amount of tears I had already shed over losing my hair could have ended the New Jersey drought. I was humiliated, embarrassed, and really pissed off. *Shit! Shit! Shit!* But regardless of the mountain of anxiety, I just couldn't do it. I couldn't shave it all off. Maybe it was that little piece of nagging hope that by some stretch of godly power I would be spared this inevitable side effect. More likely, I was just too scared. Either way, I couldn't do it. I put the sharp instruments away and cried some more.

This was my first summer at home since I was eight years old. Every previous summer was spent at sleepaway camp in the Berkshires. So, instead of volleyball, sing-a-longs, and late night raids on the boys' bunks, I spent my days studying for the SAT that I had missed months prior. In addition to my hot flashes caused by the steroid pills, New Jersey was experiencing an intense heat wave, and I was a constant ball of sweat. One day, Tina called and asked for the zillionth time why I wouldn't come over to hang out by her pool, which would have been heaven. I couldn't hold it in any longer. I burst into tears and explained myself. "What if my hair falls out while we are swimming? What if it clogs your drain? I don't want to wear the wig because it is so damn uncomfortable and hot and what if it slides off my head?" And what if... And what if... After a few seconds of silence, she said, "I'm coming right over," and hung up.

Minutes later, she entered my bedroom and took my hand. "Debbie, I don't care. Really. I love you. Put the books down, let's get some pizza and get in the pool." Tears ran down my face as I wrapped my arms around her. I exhaled. I was so scared of being rejected, of feeling embarrassed, of literally losing even more of myself, it felt safer to just hide. And the wig—the hairy ball of lies—just made me feel worse. It meant I was pretending to be the same person that I was before. But I wasn't, and the more I held on, the worse I felt. I had to let go, take a deep breath and believe I was going to be okay in this new doughy body, bloated face, skinny legs, and soon-to-be-bald head. I walked to my closet, picked up the black bathing suit I had just purchased to cover my catheter and placed the wig at the far back corner. Maybe one day I'd want to throw it on. Maybe it would serve a purpose internally or externally, but not today. We spent the rest of the summer splashing around and staying cool—a wonderful period of acceptance from a friend I will never forget.

The summer ended and my senior year of high school began. The frequent scans were showing that the grapefruit was shrinking significantly. It was working. A sense of hope emerged. *I will survive this.*

But while the inside of my body was "winning," the outside increasingly, day by day, looked like it was being pummeled to death. My sixteen-year-old body, previously thin and toned, had morphed into something out of *Close Encounters of the Third Kind.* I stood in front of the mirror and didn't recognize my reflection. My stomach was distended like I was four months pregnant and my face puffed out like a blowfish. I was forced to wear sweatpants and baggy shirts and tried to hide behind baseball caps. In the morning, for a split second, when my eyes first opened, everything seemed normal. I felt like me inside. By the time my feet hit the plush lavender carpet, the dream was over. I looked in the mirror and was horrified. No matter how often I saw my reflection, I still couldn't believe it was me. I felt awful. I looked awful. It just sucked. Plain and simple. But even when I succumbed to the physical changes and how they made me feel inside, I still needed to deal with how the outside world reacted to me.

Although I stopped looking in mirrors and avoided my reflection in store windows, I was perpetually reminded of my cancer-ness through the eyes of everyone around me. On that very first day when I walked into the medical center, the receptionist taught me what cancer looked like in someone else's eyes. It was unforgettable, and the beginning of endless identical looks. There was no escaping strangers reactions and second looks on the street. Instead of slowing down and smiling, people quickened their step. They were caught off guard by my appearance and although their reactions were appropriate, they made me feel inhuman. As the awkward glances became part of my every day, I further lost myself to the bulldozer called cancer.

Months passed. My senior year was underway. I heard how our team was doing, heard about the party on Saturday night, heard about the John Mellancamp concert I had missed, heard about the latest scandal of Katie breaking up with Jason because Jason hooked up with Denise (Katie's best friend)—I heard everything. But I sat on the sidelines watching it all. My energy level was low. So low. When friends would ask if I wanted to join them for their daily trip to the shops or the food court at the mall, I declined nearly every time. If I made it through an eight-hour day at school, I was absolutely exhausted. Not to mention shuttling back and forth to the hospital for constant blood counts to see how my red, white, and platelet cells were hanging on, sometimes with a transfusion, sometimes not. Afterwards, I needed to return home and complete my homework or study for an exam. The idea of pulling an all-nighter was inconceivable now.

Days would come and go, but the daily activities remained the same. Which hat would suit my bald head best today? What medications needed to be refilled? Which doctor was I visiting? Oncologist? Radiologist? Surgeon? Why don't we just shake the magic eight ball and find out? *I am so sick of this. Where is my life? Where is the girl who loves to dance to eighties music and bake*

Nestlé Toll House cookies while eating half the dough?
Is she dying along with the cancer cells? Yes, my life will
always be different, but I'm still Deb, right? The cancer
was killing me in more ways than one. There were dark
days that humor couldn't penetrate. I tried to hold on
but it was just so hard.

I spent the remainder of my senior year shuttling
back and forth from chemo sessions to SAT prep class,
to the ICU because I caught some infection or virus,
to radiation sessions, and then to football games where
I would cheer on my friends. Surprisingly, it wasn't
difficult to flip from patient to teenager then back
to patient. In fact, the separation was necessary. If I
had rattled off all the thoughts I had in my head, my
friends would have flipped out. *Am I going to survive*
this? Will I never fall in love? Who could love me now?
Will I never be a mother? Mortality became real—I had
transformed into an old woman in a sixteen-year-old's
body. I tried to relate when my friends would attempt
to figure out the best way to buy some beer without
age-appropriate identification, but I just couldn't access
that girl. She had left the building. My friends couldn't
understand, and I didn't expect them to. I became a
master at switching between my two worlds, and I
kept them as separate as possible. I never discussed
my treatments with my friends and didn't discuss my
regular life with the doctors. When I walked into the
chemo clinic, I mentioned my energy level or lack
thereof, my persistent symptoms of heartburn, nausea,

or headaches. When I passed through the doors of my high school, my priorities immediately shifted. I would begin sentences with, "Can you believe that Chemistry exam? It was brutal." Versus, "I'm having hot flashes and when I throw up it's a greenish-grayish color. Is that normal?" My emotional self constantly bounced back and forth as well. From 9:00 a.m. to 10:00 a.m. I internally screamed with sorrow while my friends discussed the party they attended the previous night. I was angry and resentful, wishing I could have worn that amazing emerald sweater that I never got to show off anymore. Why was I imprisoned in this body? By 11:00 a.m., however, I'd shift once again. I had seen behind the curtain and so much of what I thought was important was not. By noon, my only wish was that I could still be living on the other side, unaware, untainted, and oblivious to such grown-up concepts of life and death. Needless to say, the days, weeks and months did not pass quickly. I agonized through each treatment and kept hoping that one day I could return to my old life—whatever that entailed.

Although I never saw "the look" from my crew of girlfriends, my relationships with them inevitably started to change. I didn't have much to add to the conversation when discussing pressing matters of teenage angst, but I did have angst, nevertheless. My contribution to the social world was the outgoing message on my answering machine that said, "I got chemo yesterday, feel like shit, can't talk, speak to you in five days." Although my life seemed to be running in a different direction, I still wanted to connect. I loved my friends, but I had come to understand the social shackles of this disease. At first, I'd hear their stories of how the party on Saturday night was dramatically broken up by the police because the parents weren't home, the music was too loud, and a half-empty beer keg happened to be sitting on the kitchen floor. I waited for my opening in the conversation, but nothing came. The details of my current life weren't cool or funny. If I did utter something about my medicinal day, there was a typical, standard reaction. I'd get the look that said, "I don't know what to say. Do I look into her eyes? I don't want her to think I don't understand. But I don't understand. But I don't want her to think I don't care. I shift my weight. I smile." There was distance. I was on a completely different planet and there was nothing we could do about it. They didn't feel right laughing at my pain when I would make a joke about mortality or baldness, but all I wanted, in the whole wide world, was to connect. With my family, I felt like I had to stay strong because everyone looked like they had seen a ghost when they peered into my eyes. For some reason I thought my pain, the real pain, the kind of pain you don't die from, would kill them if they actually knew what I was feeling. It was so black, so dark, so all-consuming. I couldn't possibly let my mom, dad, brother, grandfather, or friends see that side—the depths of that kind of despair. My loved ones would say, "I'm here for you. I love you." But they were scared.

And of course they were! I was scared out of my fucking mind! *I don't want to die. I can handle the needles, chemo, and scars, but I don't want to die.* However, when asked how I was doing, I would typically respond, "It's just hard," or "The chemo is really kicking my ass." So on one hand I was a terrified teenager who desperately wanted to connect and fit in with my peers. Then on the other hand I was the patient. The chemo reservoir. I couldn't figure out how I was supposed to integrate my two identities. There was my old world, which I was still a part of, and the new one, which no one understood but me. So I kept them separate. I felt isolated when I was by myself, resentful that my friends were living the life I wanted to live, and fraudulent when I was trying to in fact be myself. There was really no one who could relate to me but me…and Bear, of course.

Chapter 3
Birth of the Mani-Pedi

MONTHS HAD PASSED SINCE my diagnosis. There wasn't a single ounce of femininity left in me. My gaunt legs held the foundation of a paunch belly and listless arms. My skin was dry and crackly and had turned a grayish hue. My friends, my old life, seemed to be drifting away. I felt isolated. Like all seventeen-year-olds I measured my self worth against my surrounding peer group, but given the utter disparity between *me* and *them*, I needed something new to use as a benchmark. When I looked in the mirror, I saw a cancer patient. I needed a reminder, an anchor, that I was still a girl.

I sat on the floor of my bedroom with my legs flexed against the floral lavender wallpaper. As I stared at my thighs and calves, I tried to remember what I used to look like. How could these legs be attached to the same person who scored the winning point on the volleyball court against Wayne Hills? *Was that a dream? Is this?* My stomach was distended and my face was blown up like a chipmunk from the steroids. With every shampoo, my hair thinned and I died a little more inside. What was happening to me? My identity was changing without my consent or permission. I was drowning. And then I saw them! I saw a tiny bit of me! A burst of fresh, healthy, multicolored air filled my lungs and gave me life again. As my mourning eyes scanned literally every inch of my body, they uncovered two parts of me that were exactly the same as they were months ago—proportion, color, tone, touch, everything. My hands and feet! They were still soft, clean, and youthful. They had not been swallowed whole by disease or chemicals. I had hoped, begged, and prayed for something to help me reconnect with myself and when my eyes landed on my hands and feet, I felt like I'd been offered a rope to pull me out of the quicksand. *Okay, if this is all I have left to make me feel sexy and healthy—well, I'm going for it.* I probably should have been studying for the SAT or reading over my history paper, but fuck it. It was time to remind myself of who I really was. I walked out of my room, opened the hallway linen closet, and unlocked the medicine cabinet where my mother kept her nail kit. There it was—the beige travel LeSportSac toiletry bag that I had seen her use a hundred times. I tore into it. There wasn't much inside because she usually went to the salon for her manicures, but I discovered a nail file, buffer, cuticle scissors, and clear nail polish. *I might be bald, I might be nauseated, but I'm sure as hell going to have beautifully manicured hands and feet.* For weeks I felt reenergized as I filed my square tips, applied clear coats of strengthener, moisturized, and pushed my cuticles back (no cutting) and lo and behold my nails grew. My body was listening to me. I felt healthy! Needless to say, this began a mani-pedi obsession. My visits to Rite Aid took on yet a new meaning. There were serious decisions to be made—should it be Drama Queen Red or Kiss My Lips Pink today? I spent hours massaging in creams and applying lacquer to reach the end result—beautifully crafted nails. I applied flowers and rhinestones; it was the early nineties after all. Sometimes just a sheer nude would do. I practiced and practiced and practiced. It was mani-pedi therapy and it was working! Some of the weight lifted. Moments of pleasure were re-infused into my predominantly nauseous existence. My mani-pedis were liberating, like taking off your panty hose after a long, laborious day. My bedroom served as my own little spa where I could clear my mind and focus on the color at hand— Pink-ing of You, My Chihuahua Bites, or Chick Flick Cherry—and the artistry that was sure to unfold.

What is it about this stuff that girls love? Is it the smell of acetone and alcohol? Is it the seemingly infinite color wheel? Why are we always curious and ask, "What color is that? I love it." We get so excited when we find a new color that is our "it" color of the season. Is it the shimmer? The silly communion with other women? The colors themselves reminded me of the splendor in life. Their vitality and variety extracted the unique part of me that was suffocating from the chemo. I was no longer the patient taking orders from the doctor. I was the master of my own destiny. *Do I want to choose the corals or the reds today?* It was up to me. The names themselves put a smile on my face and each color made me feel differently. The pinks brought out my inner princess, the Molly Ringwald in *The Breakfast Club* if you will—the proper, boarding school, conservative kind of girl: Ballet Slippers, My Way, or Sugar Daddy. The reds—look out—brought out the fiery vixen in me. The woman who holds the power. Wait, not only holds the power, but demands it: I'm Not Really A Waitress Red, Paint My Moji-toes Red, and A-List. I have to say, when the reds were on I actually leaned towards tighter jeans and higher heels. The neons, like yellows, blues, and greens, were unusual for me. I had to feel pretty funky to venture that far out of my comfort zone, but I did throw down the gauntlet every now and then. Since I couldn't attend a salon, I created one in my bedroom. Thankfully, all the bells and whistles translated with ease. With the exception of the massage chair, I could replicate pretty much all of it. And just when I thought this was merely a hobby that kept my mind off the obvious, I realized it was so much more.

A few months into my treatment, I was lying in bed, as usual, because some symptom had decided to show up unannounced like a drunken ex-boyfriend at 2:00 a.m. on a Saturday night, and I couldn't take it anymore. How many side effects could one drug have? But then, as I was about to get swallowed whole by the pernicious meds, I saw my pearly pink toes peeking out from my Laura Ashley comforter. My feet spoke: "Hello, beautiful. Take a deep breath. You might not be able to feel it right now, but trust me, you're still here." I stared reflectively at my fingernails and toes. Their strength, shine, vibrant color, and femininity all reassured me that I was still alive. *I'm still here. I still count.* Somewhere beyond all of this cancer shit, life awaits. Not this life that had consumed me over the last several months, but my real life, the life that I missed so desperately—the life of an ordinary seventeen-year-old girl who sneaks out of her mother's house to see her boyfriend, the girl who wreaks havoc at the local movie theater by throwing popcorn at her friends while getting scolded by the grown-ups behind her.

Nails, hair, and skin—they don't define us. They are not kind, gracious, sensitive, or loving. That said, when my internal self was a prisoner, when I couldn't stand to be in the same room with her, I kept looking to my exterior self for comfort. But that wasn't easy. I was devastated about my hair. My thick, brown silky hair had thinned out, lost its shine, and left bald spots. I was too embarrassed to walk to the corner store without a baseball cap, and repeatedly friends and family would say, "Deb, it's just hair. It'll grow back. Isn't the important thing that the medicine is working and you're going to get better?" *You don't understand.* I felt shot down. I was sick of people telling me that my feelings were not acceptable. *It's just hair. Why is this such a big freakin' deal? Why do I care? But I do care—so much.* I cared so much that I began to feel guilty. Sometimes I could put on a brave face and walk down the street in full post-chemo disaster, but most of the time I wanted to hide. Finding my mani-pedi gave me something to smile about, a sliver of myself that remained unchanged.

Through each side effect and the everyday ups and downs, my mani-pedi sessions were so much more than just sixty minutes of stress relief. They were my salvation. When despair took over and social anxiety reared its ugly head, I couldn't simply blow dry my hair, apply some red lipstick, throw on my leather jacket and head out the door. But I could still have perfectly polished dazzling red fingers and toes—and I felt pretty. Dare I say there were even times they made me feel sexy? *Bald & Sexy—now that would be a great nail color!* I honestly looked at my hands and saw beauty. Beauty in *me*. No matter how many pounds I gained or lost, Dazzling Diva made me feel like I could put on my best pair of sweatpants, throw on my baseball cap, and rock my body all the way to Rite Aid to shop for my weekly color (and refill my stool softener). I walked straighter and smiled wider, even if it was only for a moment. Anything that can give you that kind of confidence should be applauded. Thank you Essie. Thank you OPI. Thank you Brucci. Thank you Revlon, for giving me an outlet that inspired me, and, well, saved me.

Chapter 4

The Blonde Bulldog

THE HOSPITAL WAS ITS own small nation. There were laws of the land with specific policies, a dress code, and even its own climate. Whether I liked it or not, I had become a citizen. I have always believed that we are shaped by our environment and in turn, our environment reflects us. How are we connected? What purpose do we serve? Who relates to us? Are *you* like *me*? I entered this foreign world of linoleum floors, mechanical beds, and medicinal vocabulary without knowledge or control. The rules changed overnight and my priorities changed over time. Prior to my diagnosis, my relationships with my friends and my athletic abilities were fundamental. In my new world, there was no room for such frivolity. The oncologists were primarily concerned with my treatment. The nurses were concerned with my blood counts. The technicians were concerned with lining up my body, just right, for every scan. *So, who am I in this world?* I was a conquest, a challenge, a treatment, or procedure. I was not a girl. I was cancer. With every machine beep, IV pole, complicated dialogue between white coats, there was a not-so-invisible thread. These warriors stood beside me in battle against the Big C. It would be down to the last man standing…life vs. death. Me or the cancer. Behind closed doors, choices were made on my behalf. I was not welcome in those conference rooms. Information trickled in on a need-to-know basis. I was searching for equality, security, competency—maybe even mastery. I was 100% totally and completely confused.

I searched for balance and looked for ways to adjust to my new normal. This life mandated different priorities. I learned to be the patient who held back the tears. I tried anything my team recommended. If asked, "Are you ready?," or "Can you handle this?" the answer was always, "Yes." I strived to become the perfect patient in order to feel like an achiever, a success. But even perfect patients feel pain.

For several weeks I had been feeling aches in my ankles, hips, and knees but didn't think much about it. It was tolerable, so I dealt with it. One night around 8:00 p.m., the aches increased in severity. I had endured so many forms of pain that I figured I could handle it. I put on a brave face and held off on calling the doctor. By 10:00 p.m., the pain had increased exponentially. One phone call later, and my mother jumped into her car to pick up my newly prescribed Tylenol with codeine. She raced home, hoping to relieve my agony. I took the pills and waited. No relief. *Did I just take a painkiller or were those Skittles?* My brother was home from college for the weekend and tried to help. He cracked jokes, changed the TV channel for me, and brought me ice pops, but he couldn't distract me from the pain. By 11:00 p.m., my pillow was soaked with tears and I tried visualizing puppies and rainbows for comfort. Okay, not exactly modern medicine but I was desperate. I started to scream. Really scream. *Holy shit this hurts! This must be hell.* A neighbor heard my howling and called to make sure everything was okay. We didn't live in an apartment building. We lived in a house…in the suburbs.

By 11:30 p.m., my mother headed back to CVS to pick up something stronger, I think it was morphine. We waited thirty minutes…an hour. I felt like every bone in my body, my arms, legs, pelvis, neck, and back—were all breaking in half. My bones seemed to be cracking one by one, then miraculously healing, only to break again. By 1:00 a.m., I couldn't stand it any longer. I needed help. My mom called 911. A few minutes later, three firemen, two police officers, and three paramedics entered my 10 x 10 floral lavender nail spa. I didn't care that these strangers breached sacred ground. I was just so thankful I was going to the hospital where they could put me out of my misery.

And then the unthinkable happened. My pain subsided. Why? Because it was trumped by pure humiliation! It just so happened that Mike, the President of my high school class, volunteered for the local EMS. "Hey Deb." Huddled on my bed in my gray sweat-soaked tank top and white Jockey bikini underwear, I just thought, *Oh my God. Seriously? Am I hallucinating?* Notwithstanding the many hours of bone-breaking pain and a good bit of medication, I was unfortunately not hallucinating. There I was, lying half-naked and completely humiliated. *Screw the pain—kill me now.* I was mortified as the men carried me out of my beloved sanctuary via stretcher towards the motherland where a team of doctors and nurses could figure out what the hell was happening. But Mike was kind and didn't judge me. He smiled and sat next to me in the ambulance and validated the shitty night I was having. He didn't once mention that I was half-naked with unshaven legs and puffy eyes. (I wonder if he was at all distracted my perfectly polished toes.) We arrived at the hospital and someone pushed my gurney through the emergency entrance like we were in an episode of ER. I continued to scream at the top of my lungs. An ER tech filled a syringe with some magical potion, rolled me over, and jabbed me in the ass. Ten seconds later, I was out and it was over. Holy hell, what a night!

I arrived at my doctor's office the following Monday morning and informed him of the weekend's festivities. I described, in detail, the kind of pain that I experienced in an attempt to figure out the cause and proper protocol should it happen again. To my soul-shattering surprise, he was smug and dismissive. "Yes, Deb, bone pain is a side effect of one of the drugs you are receiving in your chemotherapy treatment."

"Bone pain? Dr. D, this was not just bone pain. This was pain to the 100th power."

"Deb, I think you're being a bit of a drama queen."

My mouth dropped. *Bastard!* I generally have a lot to say (if you haven't noticed that by now), but I was speechless. *Did this asshole just have the balls to call me a drama queen to my face after I described the worst night of my life? Maybe I should kick him where it counts with my Knockout Pout pedi!* But even though I was outraged, I kept my mouth shut. I let him diminish the experience and belittle my feelings. He was the doctor, after all. The captain in my war. But was there any reason why he couldn't fight for me and validate my feelings at the same time? Even if I had made the whole thing up and was describing pink elephants flying around the room singing "Yankee Doodle Dandy," a medical professional has no right to call a seventeen-year-old girl going through chemotherapy a drama queen. *Asshole.*

Thankfully, Dr. D was only a single man in a larger group of doctors and nurses who consistently gave me the one thing I needed more than anything—a feeling of security. I trusted my team. You can't teach this stuff at Harvard or be awarded this honor at some fancy dinner of your peers. You either have it or you don't. Most of my doctors saw *me*, a terrified, pissed-off teenager who wasn't prepared for any of the things that were happening to her. *Empathy*—it may seem simple, but it's a very big word. The intuition and medical artistry of a small group of very special people saved me a little bit each day.

They didn't only support me medically; they helped me navigate hospital land—and made me feel heard.

When spring rolled in, I only had two more chemo cycles to go. The finish line was in sight. One afternoon, I felt particularly winded as I walked up the second flight of stairs at school. By fifth-period English, I had to stop mid-hallway and lean against the lockers along the wall. *What's happening?* The bell rang and the halls cleared out. I knew something was off. I couldn't remember what normal levels of energy felt like, but even for me, this was not standard. My mother picked me up and we headed straight to the clinic. As always, with warm smiles and embraces, the nurses brought me into the exam room to check my vitals. Something was clearly wrong. My pulse oximetry (aka pulse ox) reading was way off. Pulse oximetry is the measurement of both your pulse and hemoglobin saturation. Basically, your hemoglobin (part of your blood) carries oxygen. This particular machine measures if your hemoglobin is doing a good job, or not. The nurse who administered the test looked at my number, shook her head, and said, "This must be wrong. Let me get another machine." She returned a few minutes later, repeated the test, and got the same reading. I was in respiratory distress. Ten minutes later, I was admitted to the ICU with a nasty case of pneumonia.

Everything happened so fast. The doctors pumped me full of steroids and various other drugs to help my body fight. The first night was pretty touch-and-go.

After a few critical days where life and death hung in the balance, I finally stabilized. The medications were doing their job and the staff felt like they had a handle on the pneumonia. At midnight on the fourth night, a nurse walked into my hospital room. My mother was sitting on the cot beside my bed that she'd slept in for the last three nights. The nurse informed her that I was to be moved out of the ICU onto a regular floor within the hour. My mother, a 5'4", 115-pound picture of class, politely asked to speak to the nurse in the hallway.

"What's going on?" she asked.

"We need to move your daughter. Another child needs this room."

"But is she well enough?" my mother asked.

"She'll be fine," added the nurse.

"I understand she *will* be fine but *is* she fine?" The nurse recognized that my mother was questioning their call to make this move, especially at midnight. After some politically standard responses, my mother started to lose her patience. "I am well aware that there are certain criteria required to be admitted to the ICU, as well as specific criteria to be *discharged* from the ICU. You have not given me one good reason why you are transferring my daughter in the middle of the night."

In that instant, the blonde bulldog was born. My mother took the reins and became my champion. I was very sick and she was very concerned. But we had been around the block enough times to know that someone had to take charge. Once it became obvious that my mother wasn't backing down without real information, the nurse explained that another child recently came out of the operating room and needed an ICU bed. My mom understood the bumping system.

"I understand the protocol. But my priority is Deborah. You have not convinced me that she is ready to be on a regular floor. And don't you dare think for one minute that I'm disregarding the needs of that other child coming out of the OR." Calls were made, nurses and doctors whispered behind the main desk. I was moved to a regular floor—along with all my ICU monitors and a twenty-four hour oncology nurse at my bedside.

With long exhales and an achy heart, my mom learned how to play hardball. It wasn't only my identity that was being challenged daily. She, too, needed to conform to this new world and figure out how to survive. I was so grateful to have her as my advocate when I clearly couldn't stand up for myself.

Chapter 5

Zones 1, 2, and don't forget 3

ALTHOUGH MY STUDIES OBVIOUSLY played second fiddle to my treatments during my senior year of high school, I was getting the best grades that I had ever received. I'd be lying if I said that I wasn't given special treatment. Teachers extended deadlines for me and I took exams at my dining room table while sipping chamomile tea. My treatments, and their corresponding side effects, demanded I stay home, in bed or on the couch. I couldn't attend the party of the year six weeks ago or six days ago. I didn't have the energy to talk endlessly on the phone from 9:00 p.m. to 1:00 a.m. And I certainly wasn't sneaking in and out of my house to meet a boyfriend waiting in his car around the corner. Instead, I was home and I was bored to death. Even though I was too tired to change out of my pajamas, I was alert enough to study, write, memorize, and learn. So, I did my schoolwork. And my grades matched my efforts. I guess you can call that a silver lining, right?

In January, my chemotherapy regimen finally ended. I threw myself a little internal party. I had made it.

This meant so many things: (1) no more nausea, (2) my fragile, tiny hair follicles could finally start to give birth again, and (3) my body could begin healing after ten months of poisonous cocktails that we hoped would annihilate all the cancer cells. My scans were "clean," a word I grew to love. Although I knew the answer, I asked my team whether it was really necessary to pursue the radiation regimen that was scheduled for the next four months. Their answer: "We have to stick to the plan, Deb. We decided on this protocol because of your Hodgkin's stage. Since you were 3B, we have to continue as planned—both chemo and radiation." I understood the reasoning but it was worth a shot. If the chemo didn't destroy the cancer cells, the radiation was supposed to finish them off. The one-two punch. *Fair enough.*

I was used to my chemo regimen. Every two weeks: drive to the clinic; sit in one of the ten brown barcaloungers next to some other unfortunate soul who was in for the same thing. We looked like a row of sardines, reclining with our catheters attached to IV bags while various chemo cocktails dripped into our bodies. Then, several hours later, I would return home and feel like shit for a few days while we hoped the toxins eradicated the cancerous cells. I knew the drill. But now it was over and I had to prepare for the next hurdle.

Radiation was a different beast. In some ways, it was much easier because there were fewer side effects. That said, I had to go every day—Monday through Friday for four months. *What a pain in the ass.* My body was divided into three different zones: neck, chest, and pelvis. Six weeks were dedicated to each zone. The week before my first session, I was given a tour of the radiation department and introduced to the machine that would be hovering over me, giving those lingering, microscopic cancer cells a run for their money. *Nice to meet you.* Then, Dr. D explained that I would lie down on the metal table while the technician aligned the machine in the exact same location each time so there'd be no overlap, thereby preventing extraneous radiation. In order to stay within such a precise region, little marks would need to be pierced onto my body for the technician to use as his map.

"What kind of mark?" I innocently asked.

"We tattoo you," he responded.

"You what?"

He explained that they use tiny marks the size of a pencil prick. I thought about it for a second and said, "Umm... No." I was so tired of being told what to do, what to wear, what to eat, when to sleep—I was sick of it all. And now they wanted to puncture my body and leave a permanent mark? *Not happening.* I didn't care how small the little marks would be. The fact that they were permanent was too much for me to bear. I just wanted to get through the radiation and move on with my life. I had already endured surgeries and scars, and as minimal as the little black dots might be,

I didn't want any more permanent reminders of my battle with cancer. I pleaded: "Is there any other option? Anything?"

Annoyed by my request, Dr. D explained that he could mark my body with a permanent marker and create a massive grid for the technician to follow. However, this would entail washing my body with a washcloth for the next four months and never being able to shower since the marker would smudge or wash off. Without a second thought, I agreed. He repeated, "Deb, no showers. Sponge baths only…for four months." "Yes, I understand." I hopped up on the table as Dr. D and two techs stretched measuring tapes over my torso and drew thick, purple lines across my body. One said, "39 left." The other, "65 right." And then the line was drawn from one dot to the other. When I left, my chest looked like the floor plan of the Empire State Building.

A few days later, I woke up at 6:00 a.m., quickly threw on the clothes hanging over my desk chair, and drove to the hospital for my daily RT session. The technician carefully aligned the machine directly over the purple grid. At this point I was no stranger to the fact that when the red light started to blink, I would be the only one left in the room. I understood the whole radiation thing, that the technicians needed to protect themselves from being zapped fifty times a day, but the reality didn't help my adolescent identity crisis. *What is wrong with me? They can't even stay in the room with me?* I was scared. For about twenty minutes the invisible rays penetrated my body and, we hoped, eradicated any remaining cancer cells. This day was to repeat itself eighty-two times.

Each zone came with its own side effects. Zone 1, my abdominal region, caused immediate nausea. No matter how many anti-nausea drugs I took, I spent at least an hour over the toilet after every session. Since French class was my first period of the day, I ended up accumulating quite a few tardy points during those six weeks. Finally, when Zone 1 ended and Zone 2 commenced, the nausea stopped, thank God. Zone 2 zapped my neck. It only took a few days for radiation burns to penetrate the thin, supple skin of the entire region. It was like a bad sunburn—not such a big deal. But the rays also seared off the virgin hairs that were desperately trying to grow back from my ears down to the nape of my neck. As you might expect, I was less than thrilled. Then, when we were about to begin radiating the third and final section, my pelvic region, we were met with quite a surprise.

One afternoon, my mother and I were asked to report to a floor we'd never been to, which was funny because we thought we'd seen every inch of the hospital. I had completed twelve weeks of radiation to my chest and neck and we were down to the last six weeks. *It's almost over. I'm so close!* My mother and I giggled as we walked through the hallways, discussing my plans for the summer and my excitement about college, which started in just a few short months. It felt so good to see her smile. I had endured so much of this battle and I was still standing. I walked through the hospital thinking, *I've got this.*

We arrived at our destination assuming this would be the pelvic part of the tour. A man walked into the room looking dapper and suave. *Who is this guy?* He began with, "Hi, I'm Dr. V. Deb, you're about to endure radiation treatment to your pelvis region." *Yep.* "You are seventeen-years-old and we need to think about your future and the fact that you might want to become a mother one day. This radiation treatment has the potential to cause irreparable damage to your ovaries, enough to possibly put you into early menopause. There's a procedure that we can perform to prevent that from happening. We would suture your ovaries together and then place a magnetic field over them to protect them from the radiation." My eyes bulged. *Excuse me? Wait just one second…surgery?* He explained that the procedure would be similar to what they do in the dentist's office when they take X-rays of your mouth and cover your chest with the heavy bib. It took a moment for the shock of his words to sink in. When it had, I shouted, "What? You guys are just bringing this up now?" *Ugh! I thought I was in the home stretch. Why can't they just leave me alone?*

On the way home, my mom pulled over and turned to me. "Deborah, this is your decision. You're turning eighteen in a few weeks and this is your life. Whatever you decide, I will support you." The tears started to fall. I wasn't scared—death was pretty much the only thing that actually scared me at this point—but I was unprepared for yet another hurdle. I felt sucker punched, like I was perpetually knocked down, and then expected to just get back up. My internal coach was saying, "C'mon, get up!" But the fighter icing her bloody lip in the corner of the ring was saying, "Just leave me the fuck alone!" It took a few days, but I decided to trudge ahead with the full-blown treatment—no blocking. I understood the risks, but I also had a crystal clear focus on one goal: survival. If there was the tiniest chance that a microscopic cancer cell could possibly hide behind my ovary and gain protection by that magnetic field, I would never forgive myself. Even though I wanted to be a mom one day, I was completely exhausted, and my body had been through too much to take that chance. I just hoped like hell that my ovaries would hold out. Six weeks later, the radiation ended. *Break out Essie's Dancing in the Isles— my fingers and toes want to celebrate!*

Nine months of chemo: check. Eighteen weeks of radiation: check. My arduous journey, filled with missed school days, make up exams, nauseated mornings, awkward hallway stares, hospitalizations, surgeries, and scars: worth every minute. There were only two weeks until my graduation. On June 24, 1994, I woke up, and shimmied into a plum body-hugging sundress that draped to the floor. With buttons down the front and new silver accessories, I almost didn't care that my hair had barely started to grow back and that I looked like a hard-core rocker chick. Maybe it wasn't a look that I'd pick for myself given other alternatives, but it was certainly a look. Maybe it didn't match my personality or suit my face, but I didn't care. The most important thing was that it didn't spell cancer patient. My mother and I worked so damn hard to get to this day. When I took the stage in the middle of the football field and the principal called my name, I looked up into the bleachers and found my mom. She was filled with pride. I felt strong for the first time in a long time.

Chapter 6
Find Me Eisner

IT WAS THE SUMMER of 1984 and I had just turned eight. My parents decided to send my brother and me to sleepaway camp for one month. I tried using my best manipulation tactics to convince them that it was a horrible idea. I cried, begged, and pleaded, but they wouldn't budge. We were going. We drove into the school parking lot where the coach buses lined up. The counselor, wearing a torn David Bowie T-shirt, was shouting over the commotion of tear-filled goodbyes and excited enthusiasm: "Trunks in the bottom of the bus and then wait for your name to be called before you board!" There were kids with boundless energy running around the parking lot with water guns. My brother and I were thinking, *What are they so excited for? This is awful.* I was already homesick. The counselor called my name. I hugged my mom and dad and followed the other children onto the bus. Once I found my seat, I scanned the bus trying to locate my brother, my only saving grace. *Where is Robert?* I looked out the window and saw my father banging on the door of our station wagon. My brother had locked himself in the car and refused to come out! Before I knew it, the bus's engine started to rumble. My palms suctioned themselves to the glass window as my parent's car, with brother inside, disappeared. Thankfully, two teenage girls saw the utter fear in my eyes, and graciously comforted me during the three-hour journey up to the Berkshires. My father ended up driving my brother to camp that night, and I finally saw Robert the next day at the waterfront. Despite his presence, I was horribly homesick that first summer. I sent letters to my parents describing how miserable I was. I cried myself to sleep at night, moped around for hours, and refused to participate in instructional swim. I never could have guessed that for many summers thereafter, camp would be, well, magical.

Eisner was originally the estate of a very wealthy family. A sprawling mansion sits on many acres of rolling hills with the Berkshire Mountains serving as its magnificent backdrop. Marble statues are present around every corner. A beautifully crafted white and gray marble dock juts out onto a serene lake. Legend has it that the original owner was a wealthy businessman. His daughter, stricken with illness and wheelchair bound, was an art lover, and since she could not travel to see the world's magnificent pieces, he used his resources to transport the statues home where she could enjoy them at her leisure. I don't know if the legend is true, but we all believed it, and it made Eisner's beauty all the richer. The small lake used for swimming and boating was situated on the front end of the property. It was great for those balmy, ninety-degree days when ice cubes melted in seconds. But once the satisfying coolness wore off, my friends and I would quickly realize why we hated swimming in the lake. As soon as our feet touched the bottom, the slimy, slippery mush had us shuddering with disgust. We tried our best to tread water so the gunk wouldn't get between our toes.

By ten years old, I'd fallen in love. Camp days were packed with sports, art, drama, canteen, boating, swimming, singing, and eating. I loved my friends, the mountains, ga-ga, color war, campfires, and the camaraderie between campers. By twelve, another element of Eisner entered the picture. I had the sudden urge to punch Brian Levine while simultaneously wishing he would pay attention to me during song session in the dining hall. What was happening to me? What was swirling around in my stomach? Whatever it was, it was powerful. Each summer, after the counselors went to bed, my friends and I would peer out our bunk windows and eagerly watch the older campers—thirteen, fourteen, and fifteen-years-old—tiptoe out of their bunks as they made their way to the boys' side of the hill. What could possibly be so important that they risked getting caught by a counselor and getting in trouble, or, even worse, sprayed by a skunk at 2:00 a.m.? Great lengths were taken to reach the boys' side of camp—and then what? My eight, nine, ten-year-old heart just didn't understand. But that summer, the summer after I turned twelve, it all became clear.

I began to notice boys and they began to notice me. I'm not sure what it was about Eisner that lent itself to pubescent revelry. Maybe it was the 24/7 activity, whether it was soccer or dance, between boys and girls. Maybe it was staring up at the stars, night after night, connecting to a world greater than video games and MTV, which consumed our lives back in the real world. Maybe it was the safety we felt in our surroundings that let us experience these natural, yet totally terrifying feelings. Whatever the reason, my girlfriends and I were soon totally obsessed with the opposite gender. We made lists of the cutest boy, the smartest, the sweetest, the most athletic, the one with the best handwriting, and so on. Boys, boys, boys. And then my dreams came true. Michael C., who I had thought was totally cute, told his best friend, who told my best friend, who told me, that he liked me. He *liked me* liked me. That night, once he got confirmation that I was in fact also crushing on him, he came up to me after dinner and took my hand. We walked around the dining room during dessert (which was the most privacy we could get when we were twelve years old), giggling and talking. We were officially considered "together."

That night was the first time a boy's lips touched mine. It was the perfect kiss. I ran back to my bunk to tell my friends and tried not to lose my shit with excitement. I couldn't stop smiling and felt so grown up. Now, to clarify, this was a closed-mouth kiss—no tongue action. A week—and many kisses—later, a rumor was traveling around our unit that we were going to have our first co-ed campfire and sleepover. *Holy crap!* I was so excited I couldn't stand it. I actually had a boyfriend to share this incredible experience with. I felt so mature. As the days approached, the sweet kisses outside the dining room after mealtime turned a corner. I knew Michael wanted more. The day of the sleepover, right before instructional swim at 9:00 a.m., he asked me if I was ready to really kiss him. Although some of my friends had already taken the plunge and allowed a boy to stick their wet, slimy tongue in their mouth, I wasn't ready. I still thought it was an absolutely horrific idea. *Yuck. Why on earth would I want to do that?* I cared for Michael. I made that clear, but I told him I wasn't ready.

Later, my friends and I packed our cutest pajamas and rolled up our sleeping bags ready for an incredible, life-changing evening. There was an unfortunate thunderstorm that night, but that didn't disappoint sixty twelve-year-old boys and girls. We took cover in one of the activity halls. As we walked into our first co-ed slumber party, Rachel grabbed my arm and pulled me to the back of room. She began to whisper in my ear... My heart sank. Rachel told me that Michael had just dumped me and that he was planning to share his sleeping bag with Jennie Cohen! I was utterly humiliated, but I refused to let it show. I was confused and hurt. There were so many feelings. *What just happened? Am I not good enough? Not pretty enough? Not thin enough? Not endowed enough? Not popular enough? Not funny enough?*

The next morning I heard that he and Jennie Cohen had gotten to second base. *Okay, I get it. I'm not loose enough.* Thus began my understanding of the differences between love and lust. I was only twelve, so I didn't spend much conscious time analyzing the event. However, one thing was clear to me. I'd made the right decision. I wasn't ready and no one was going to pressure me into doing something with my body that I wasn't prepared to do. That summer passed and so did many other boy sagas. Seth liked me, but I didn't like him. I liked Marc, but he didn't like me. Around and around we went.

Those first few years of adolescence were filled with late-night phone calls, break-ups, and make-ups. My heart would race as I waited by the phone. He said he was going to call tonight. Sometimes he would, sometimes he wouldn't. My thirteenth, fourteenth, and fifteenth birthdays passed, and my experience with boys progressed with age. I was no longer disgusted by the contact sport of Danielle Steele or Jackie Collins kissing marathons.

I had my first actual boyfriend at fifteen. His name was Jason, and he was a sweetheart. We were together for several months in a committed, serious relationship. We laughed, supported and leaned on each other. We hooked up like any red-blooded teenage couple, but he was well aware that I wasn't ready to move to higher ground—well, lower ground, actually. There wasn't much else to talk about regarding that subject. It wasn't a negotiation. I had watched all of those After School Specials discussing the dangers of STDs and pregnancy. Quite frankly, I was scared shitless. I wasn't even remotely prepared to be in the same room with words like *gonorrhea* or *fetus*. One Thursday night in March, when I was sitting at my dining room table preparing for a geometry exam, the kitchen phone rang. I smiled when I heard Jason's voice. We hadn't spoken in twelve hours—in teenage time, an eternity. His voice deepened and without pause, he confessed that he'd had sex with his lab partner. I was hurt. I was numb. I couldn't understand why sex and love served completely different functions. I thought they were supposed to be intertwined. I reflected back to those adolescent years at Eisner. *Of course, dumbass. These are teenage boys.* Months later I was diagnosed with Hodgkin's Disease, and the love/sex part of my life became less than even a passing thought. I had no choice but to focus on survival while my friends continued experiencing their dramatic sagas of lovers and cheaters. I knew I had to be patient and hoped I'd be lucky enough to eventually rejoin the fun. The heart-wrenching, dramatic, crazy rite of passage. I waited, endured, and finally my time came.

The summer between high school graduation and the fall of my freshman year, I returned to my beloved alma mater as a camp counselor. It felt like the perfect antidote to my fucked up year of chaos and pain. Eisner always made things better.

As I stared out the window on the bus up to the Berkshires, the trees and memories passed by. It was the same route I'd taken year after year, a beautiful drive up the Taconic Parkway. I was eight years old when I spent my first summer at Eisner. It was hard to believe a decade had elapsed. Driving through the gates was like a homecoming—everything looked the same. The bus pulled up to a crossroads, the center of camp, and I set foot on the rustic gravel roads. I was immediately greeted by an old friend. Alex stood before me, his face alight with a smile. Two years before, our friendship gave way to something more intimate, but our adolescent affair was short-lived, given that we lived eight hours apart. It had been a year since I'd seen him. Probably two since our last kiss. Within days, Alex made it clear that he was ready to pick up where we left off. What was he thinking? Couldn't he see? I was broken. My feelings were buried deep, underneath the two millimeters of hair that had made their maiden voyage out of my scalp. Beneath the fading radiation burns, there was a girl who Alex had never met.

"Deb, can I see you tonight?"

"I'm not sure, Alex."

"What do you mean? We've been at camp for two weeks. I'm practically begging at this point. You know how I feel about you. I know how you feel about me. I can see it."

While my stomach felt like an erupting volcano, I held his hand and said, "I know you can see it. I do care about you," and then turned around before the rest of the sentence spilled out of my mouth—*But the girl you think you see is long gone, and every time you look at me, it reminds me of who I'm not.*

By the third week I couldn't do it anymore. It was the night of the camp-wide scavenger hunt—an event that every camper (and counselor) looked forward to. While I tagged along with my girlfriends and their campers, searching for hidden clues in Bunk 11 and on the softball field, I felt my hand being pulled.

"Give me one reason. One reason we can't be together," Alex pressed. Between the security of Eisner and the fondness I felt for him, I surrendered.

"I don't have one." Alex kissed me and for a moment I let myself be kissed. He looked at me the way I wanted to feel—sexy, feminine, funny, and loved. *Maybe this is enough? Maybe his feelings will be powerful enough to transform me? Maybe if I hold on tight, she'll reemerge?* So eventually, reluctantly, I succumbed to his devotion and let one day take me into the next.

During the day, I'd care for the kids in my bunk, take them to their activities, smear them with sunblock, and relish their enjoyment of this magical place called Eisner. In the evenings, I'd do my best to fit in with Alex and my friends, the same friends that seemed like family. But as I roasted marshmallows and sang James Taylor songs by firelight, my heart ached. *Is the cancer going to come back? Will I ever feel safe? Will these people attend my funeral? Will I ever feel good about myself again?* I didn't want to die. Even more significantly, I wanted to live. I wanted to live without these fears, without this past. My heart and body whispered constant reminders that I was now different, but I desperately wanted to be the same old idealistic girl who ran through the lawn with her friends singing camp songs. I wanted to be her so badly. It was one thing to feel alone in high school—a place where many tortured souls feel isolated. But at Eisner? Never.

And so began an especially toxic cycle in my life. I suppressed my feelings of self-loathing, of being damaged goods, and began to subconsciously sabotage every relationship I had. Alex and I had been together for the entire summer and I knew I couldn't go on with this deceit. I felt like a fraud when he looked into my eyes and I knew I was not the girl he thought I was. I had to end it, but how? I had no strength. I had no truth. Camp was almost over and while I would be packing up for South Jersey, he would be heading to Boston. It was our day off and about ten of us decided to drive out to the lake nearby. I decided the time had come. Drowning in anxiety, confusion, and loss, I poured myself a glass of wine, and then another. Lying on the grass, staring at the stars and discussing the excitement of independence, someone decided it was a good idea to light up a joint. I was already a bit dizzy from the couple of glasses of boxed wine that I thought would loosen me up for this dreaded conversation, but peer pressure gave way, and I inhaled. About thirty minutes later I took Alex's hand, walked us away from the crowd and told him it was over. When he asked, "Why?" I opened my mouth and without warning proceeded to throw up all over his khaki shorts and Grateful Dead T-shirt. It was definitely over. I wish I could have felt worthy of his love or seen myself through his eyes. It would have made the rest of my journey a lot easier.

Chapter 7

Alpha Beta

IT WAS FINALLY HERE. My dreams were coming true. I said good-bye to my life as a cancer patient and began a new identity as a college freshman. It was supposed to be that simple. Everyone asked, "So, you're done, right? It's over?" I focused on my new life as a regular girl, and I bottled up everything associated with the year from hell. The Hodgkin's was gone, but it had left a void the size of the Grand Canyon in the middle of my identity. Although I was irrevocably different, I refused to admit it changed me. It was just easier to say, "Yes, it's over."

A few weeks before my first day as a freshman at Rutgers, I received the anxiously awaited letter with the name and phone number of my soon-to-be college roommate. I had heard nightmare stories about clingy, annoying girls who would rattle on about their love for frozen yogurt until 2:00 a.m., or kick you out of your room for some privacy with the latest hallway hunk by hanging a scarf on the doorknob. The placement was a crapshoot. I held my breath as I opened the letter and read her name over and over again. *Is Karen the name of a girl who is kind? Will she keep a tidy room? Will she light my hair on fire in the middle of the night? Who is this girl and what will we think of each other?* I picked up the phone and dialed. She answered and said, "Hey-lo-oo." I giggled. First, we introduced ourselves. Then, the investigation began. As teenage girls, we were fully aware that all descriptive words were going to be used to categorize us. The exchange commenced: "I play volleyball, my parents are divorced, I live with my mother, my older brother is in college, and I love chocolate." She proceeded to tell me that she lived with her father, her older sister had graduated from Rutgers, and she drove a neon blue Jeep with fluorescent blinking light bulbs that outline her personalized license plate. *I love it!* She was a sweet girl from central Jersey. She then told me that her mother passed away not that long ago. I paused and ached. *Her mom?* I felt her pain.

Something happens when a friend or even mere acquaintance invites you into her personal story. It opens the door for you to meet their generosity and trust them with your own sad saga. Vulnerabilities are matched and hence, you can open up. Karen gave me the courage to speak. I fearfully began to blurt out things like "cancer," "It's called Hodgkin's," and "I am fine now." I was so afraid of rejection, of feeling alone. *Is she going to hang up? Is she going to request a different roommate? Why am I telling her all of this?* But Karen didn't hang up. Instead, she invited me further into her world. "My mother died of breast cancer." I ached for her loss and the crater left by that gruesome disease. Then, surprisingly, I felt relief. Karen wasn't scared of me or my story. Like me, she knew pain and fear all too well. Our conversation moved back to the journey ahead, and we giggled with excitement about sharing this new adventure together. We both silently understood that while we divulged our personal kryptonite to one another, our stories were no one else's business. We knew that darkness could penetrate at any time, but we were eighteen-year-old college freshman who wanted to feel free and experience this special stage of our lives.

Days later, just three months after my final radiation treatment, I loaded up my navy blue Toyota Camry and drove down to New Brunswick, New Jersey. My mother helped me unpack my clothes and toiletries, including two new polish bottles called Vivacious Violet. I had applied a couple of coats of the purple-red the night before, hoping it would boost my courage. Mom made my bed and organized all of my stylish new pillows and untainted collegiate paraphernalia around my half of the room. She looked at me proudly as she hugged me goodbye. "Well, you're all set. I love you, darling. Call me tonight." I felt her excitement for me as I was about to embark on this deserved adventure, but something was also awry. I knew the next four years were supposed to be filled with romance, heartbreak, parties, laughter, and new memories, but as I sat there cradled by my new fuchsia comforter, part of me wished I was somewhere else. I longed for the infusion suite with my nurses and my doctors. I was in a new world—a world I had dreamt of my whole life: college, free of doctors and medicine—yet now that I was here, I was craving the safety of those sterile hospital walls. *What the hell is wrong with me? Shouldn't I be happy that chemo is over?* Yes, I was elated that the pain of treatment was over, but, shockingly, I also wanted to return to the trenches, the IV poles and needle sticks. I had spent so much time leaning on my medical team and using them as my crutch, I didn't know what to do without them. I needed to feel like the cancer was still being fought. But the physical fight was over—the medicine was done. *So now what? Am I supposed to just sit here and wait for it to come back? Or not?*

As the sun went down that first night, I sat in my bed while everyone on the dorm floor gathered in the common room for card games and drinking contests. I heard laughter and flirting and the clinking of bottles. Friendships began to form under the guise of likeness. I understood that cancer hadn't stolen all of me over the past year and a half, but even so, I was paralyzed. *Where is the girl who takes risks and isn't afraid of anything? Why am I so terrified?* I was filled with fear. Fear of someone finding out my dirty little secret; fear of being ostracized for having a hairstyle that could only be compared to a brunette version of Little Orphan Annie's; fear of everyone finding out I was damaged goods; fear of living this life in three-month installments before my next CAT scan and, last but not least, fear of the cancer coming back. As my mind raced with these cyclical thoughts, the door burst open and Karen walked in. While everyone else was running up and down the halls like maniacs, we exchanged smiles and hugged. I sighed. Even though Karen proved to be trustworthy and didn' t judge me, I didn't have the confidence that others would follow suit. Although it's common knowledge cancer is not contagious, I still felt like people would want to run from me.

That first week of orientation was filled with introductions and categorizations. Teenagers naturally separate their peers into classes. As every John Hughes film illustrates, teens classify themselves in order to make sense of the world around them, then they attempt to find their place amidst the chaos. Are you a cheerleader, jock, nerd, punk, funny guy, or artist? These labels are generally based on external factors—maybe it's the outfit someone's wearing or the car they are driving. As superficial as it seems, the labeling helps us adjust to the pressure and conflicting nature of adolescence. In my hometown, there was no escaping my reality— the radiation burns, the hair loss—but college was a clean slate. I didn't need to talk about cancer, treatment, prognosis, symptoms, or death. *I can be anybody here. I am anonymous.* However, the pressing question was: who would I decide to be? If the girl I used to see in the mirror died, but I refused to be the girl now standing in her shoes, who the hell was I? The only thing I knew for sure was that I didn't want to be "Cancer Girl." I considered all of the things that make us who we are. On the outside, it's our face, hair, body type, and skin color. On the inside, our kindness, maturity, humor, intellect, and self-assuredness. For me, at that point, it felt like every one of these self-defining factors had been put into a blender and shredded to pieces. I didn't have the foresight or strength to realize that I needed time to put the pieces of myself back to together. So, I started from scratch. *I'm going to be the fun girl—the one who seemingly has nothing to hide.*

A few weeks into my first semester, two baseball players down the hall, Coby and Ryan, invited Karen and me over for a game of hearts. Within minutes, Karen was laughing and joking with the boys. I wasn't saying much.

"What's wrong with you? Why are you being so quiet?" Karen whispered.

"Nothing," I said. It was the boys. I was scared. What if I opened my mouth and nothing came out?

"Deb, you're being boring!" Coby called out.

"No I'm not! I'm trying to play the game—and win."

Ryan chimed in and said, "Why don't we get some drinks going in here?" While he and Coby opened a new bottle of Absolut, Karen and I took the elevator downstairs to the lobby to get a few bottles of orange juice from the vending machine. While riding back up, Karen asked, "What's going on with you?"

"I don't know," I said. "I'm just nervous around those guys."

"Just be yourself Deb. You're great."

Be myself?

Although I had dabbled with alcohol in high school, I was never a big drinker. I was accustomed to nursing Very Berry wine coolers and had never tried hard liquor before. When we returned with the mixers, there were four shot glasses filled with vodka on the floor surrounding the card game. *It looks like water. How bad can it be?* I chugged it down—my throat was on fire. Coby handed me the bottle of orange juice and I swigged it back. "Whoa!" I exclaimed.

"Yeah, it's good, right?" he said.

"If good means absolutely putrid, then yeah, it's delicious," I said.

As we turned the cards over and continued to play, more shots were poured. Karen and I took a second trip down to the vending machine.

"You seem better, Deb. Are you having fun?" she asked.

"I'm doing great."

A few card games in, I was winning. In every sense of the word. *This is amazing! I feel so good!* My confidence hadn't seen the light of day for over a year and it was back. *I'm not letting this go.* Unfortunately, I spent the next morning with my head in my black and pink polka dot garbage can and I never made it to Calculus. But it seemed like a small price to pay for such a transformation. *I think I found something here.*

A few weeks later, I decided to join a sorority. I participated in rush, and ultimately decided on the sisterhood of Alpha Beta. AB was founded by a group of young women in 1896 at the State Female Normal School in North Carolina who wanted to change the "woman's world." The patron Goddess, Hestia—the virgin goddess of the hearth, home, and chastity—represents AB, which is pretty ironic given that not all AB sisters were so chaste. The Rutgers chapter added its Jersey imprint on the southern driven sisterhood, but one thing was certain—the gals, Northern or Southern, East Coast or West, rallied to support each other. It was obvious from my first encounter that these women had each other's backs, and that was the prevailing reason I chose them.

Over the next several months, my pledge sisters and I devoted all of our spare time to our new family. These women were boisterous and funny. Some were supermodel gorgeous, some not. Some were smart as a whip, some not. Jen B. was tall, thin, and blonde. As beautiful as she was, her kindness and gentle nature shined just as bright. She never had too many drinks at the bar because she wanted to ensure everyone else's safety and ability to walk home at 2:00 a.m. Brooke was a pint-size cracker jack—athletic, strong, and so damn funny. She loved practical jokes and throwing water balloons off the house balcony in the middle of winter. I admired Jen C. from day one. She always had her nose in a book. Monday through Friday, she sat in her spot in the dining room for hours and hours, but come Saturday night, she shook it loose along with the rest of us. These girls were special in many ways, but the draw for me was their ability to let go and enjoy each moment with laughter. I dreamt of fitting in and connecting with these new women. *Would they accept me? Did they think I looked different? Did they think I was funny and kind?*

After months of pledging and going through the sisterhood's rites of passage, there were only a few days left before initiation day. They called it "hell week," but compared to the urban legend, the days were filled with silly errands and assignments, like not being able to wear make-up or nail polish! The last night of hell week, we were kidnapped in our pajamas and brought to one of the upperclassman's homes. We were escorted into the basement. It was dark and a bit scary, but as soon as my big sister Julia winked at me, I felt safe. Bernadette started to speak and we listened. She told us our final pledge challenge was about trust. We were going to follow in our sisters' footsteps and commemorate this time by drinking a goldfish. *What?!* Yes, a live, swimming, pooping, stinky, slimy goldfish. Bernadette reached over to the table and picked up a glass where we all dreadfully watched little Goldie swim round and round, and with one swig, Bernadette shot it down her throat. A few of us started to giggle with fear. *Did she really just do that? And now I'm going to?* Julia stood next to me and kept repeating, "Remember, this is about trust." Then the blindfolds came out and when everything was completely black, we were each given our own cups. I smelled it. *I shouldn't have done that.* It was fishy and nasty and there was no way I could drink. Julia repeated, "Don't worry. It's okay." And then, Bernadette counted to three. One, two, three—I pinched my nose with my left hand and tilted the cup with my right. Gross! After washing it down with water, we were allowed to take off our blindfolds. Surprisingly, no one threw up. Bernadette smiled as she told us hell week was over. Oh, and that we just swallowed tuna fish oil spiked with a mandarin orange.

I will never forget the night of my initiation. We arrived wearing white dresses, white shoes, white nail polish and our pledge pins placed perfectly above our hearts. As we lined up waiting for the doors to open, my heart raced. I was part of a team again. I had lost that camaraderie when I was shipped off to the hospital and separated from my high school friends. Thereafter, my team wore lab coats and carried stethoscopes rather than pocketbooks or backpacks. But I was back in the land of the living and they had brought me into their fold. *This feels right. I belong here.* My thoughts gave way to tears of joy and relief. When the doors opened, we were escorted inside one by one. *I am alive.* I was thankful to be experiencing something other than sorrow and pain. *I feel happy!* Although the rituals remain a secret, I don't think that I'm breaking any fraternity rules by telling you that there is an incredibly special power inherent in the gathering of one hundred women, all dressed in white, joined together hand in hand and singing songs that have been sung through the ages to commemorate loyalty and sisterhood. And then, when the initiation was complete, we broke out the shots, unbeknownst to our advisors, of course.

I fell in love with my crew of girls. We laughed at the same jokes, shared similar interests, and believed in trust, warmth, and loyalty. I was home. Days, weeks, and months passed. We grew closer and built a unit that I was an essential part of.

One night, as we were getting dressed for a formal, Trish turned to me. "Deb, I've never asked you what that scar is from?" My worlds collided. I froze in panic. My avoidance of the subject had been just that—avoidance. But now, I was at a crossroads. Should I share my past with my friends and risk jeopardizing the fun we've been having applying eye shadow and body glitter, or should I out-right lie?

"Oh, I had pneumonia once. It's a surgery scar." *What the hell just came out of my mouth?* I wasn't even making sense. There was no turning back. I'd created my story and I would have to stick with it. As women, we share, we confide. But I couldn't open up. There was too much to lose. What did it mean that I couldn't share my medical history? I didn't want to think about it. And while it was never my intention, my vow of silence quickly turned into deception. When asked about my ridiculous hairstyle, I laughed and said, "Oh, isn't it funky. I wanted to try something different." I created excuses when I had to leave school for my three-month check-up of blood tests and scans. Everyone believed me. And after telling the same story twenty times, I almost believed myself. With each new act of deception, I sank deeper into an abyss of self-hatred. But the party went on and my shame got an invite. Every little secret built on the last. I was hiding part of myself. A huge part actually. And the longer I hid, the deeper I dug myself into a hole. I wanted to have the confidence to own my past and wear it on my sleeve. And some part of me believed there was a chance I would have been pleasantly surprised to find that people accepted me, cancer and all. But I just couldn't risk it. My endless fear of being ostracized kept the truth at bay, while my self esteem took quite a beating. I was convinced there was something wrong with me. I sank deeper. If I let myself think, for a second, about the bald girl who was scared to die, I broke into a sweat and felt like I could faint. So I lied about the scars on my body all the while creating new scars that were manifesting as a black hole expanding inside me. The more I pretended to be someone else, the more I hated myself. Embarrassed and ashamed for being anything but grateful, I was left feeling isolated, abandoned and resentful.

College parties, unknown to the authorities, were filled with beer pong, ice-block shots, quarters, round the world—you name it, we did it. The opportunity to fill my cup was everywhere. And it didn't take much coercion for me to start sipping the cute little test tubes filled with blue and pink liquids. They tasted like Fun Dip—delicious! And best of all, twenty minutes later, it was like I walked into a time machine, adjusted the dials to March, 1993, and I was back to the girl who felt whole. *Hello, doll.* Like most people who finish off a cocktail, my insecurities and inhibitions melted away with each candy flavored drink. I was hooked. And in the beginning, it was worth every hangover.

My life in the sorority was non-stop merrymaking—fundraisers, mixers, dinners, semi-formals, formals, meetings, sleepovers, pranks, and jokes. I consciously sought out an environment filled with women, searching for true friendship because I wanted to connect. I loved trying on lip gloss and puckering our lips in the mirror together, shopping for mini skirts, and dancing till dawn. But when I grew silent in moments of reflection or sorrow, and my friends would ask, "What's wrong?" I couldn't respond. I genuinely couldn't ask for help. I didn't know how. I didn't even know what was wrong. Everything was moving way too fast. I was on the train and couldn't get off. I had joined this community hoping that it would consume me and turn me into its spawn. I wanted to feel powerful and pretty and happy. By the end of my freshman year, I had almost tricked myself into believing that it had worked.

Chapter 8
The Scare

THE SUMMER BETWEEN FRESHMAN and sophomore year marked my first year of survivorship. Two weeks before my return to the sorority house, I went to the hospital for my scheduled checkup. I was greeted with huge hugs from my extended family of doctors and nurses. My new world was characterized by final exams, socials, and football games. But in a single instant, I was back. I undressed, folded my clothes neatly on the stool in the corner of the exam room, and put on the white and blue exam gown I knew all too well. The Jersey girl took off her jewelry, platform shoes, and quasi-fashionable outfit—everything was stripped away except the Going Incognito polish lacquered to my fingernails. *Here I am again. The girl in the gown. What am I worth?* I tried to distract myself but nothing worked. I inhaled and exhaled. I studied my body that had withstood a war. *Who am I?* I was bare, scared, changed, and still figuring this crazy shit out. I walked out of the room, and while I caught everyone up on the fun I was having, the needles were inserted, blood was drawn, and scans snapped. We embraced, and I walked out the door leaving that life behind once again.

Twenty-four hours later, as I was organizing my clothes into piles, the phone rang. "Hello," I answered.

"Deb?"

"Hi," I responded, recognizing the voice of one of the nurses I had come to know and love over the years. She spoke slowly.

"Deb, you and your mom need to come in. We found something on your chest X-ray from yesterday. Can you come today?"

The blood drained from my face and extremities. Then my body quickly turned to autopilot. I responded with almost a whisper, "Yes, we're coming now." And we did. Over the next few hours, we listened as our situation was explained to us. In a nutshell, my doctor saw another shadow in my chest.

"The Hodgkin's is back," he said.

I had no time to process. The next day, I was admitted to the hospital where I was to undergo a surgical biopsy of the mass in my chest wall. The doctor also planned to insert a new catheter in expectation of my upcoming chemotherapy treatments. I was sternly told that the treatment administered last time was "a cake walk" compared to the toxins I would have to ingest this next time around. *Fabulous. Just fucking fabulous.*

During my previous course of treatment I was given the choice between two different kinds of catheters. Now, this is a very general, limited, Sesame Street explanation of a complicated medical device, so please take it as such. The first catheter is called a portocath. It's an internal catheter that acts as an access point for all blood work, in and out, as well as treatments. It feels like one of those tiny bouncy balls (the ones that live in the toy machine outside the diner that seven-year-olds beg their parents for while waiting for their pancakes) inside your chest. You see a little bulge coming out of your skin. The nurse jams the biggest fucking needle you have ever seen into this ball which connects to one of the main arteries in your neck. The second catheter option is a Broviac. It's the external version. The Broviac has two straw-like tubes connected to the same artery, but instead of accessing it through a needle, the tubes hang out of your chest. Thus, they can be accessed easily—at any time—with little to no pain. There are pros and cons to both devices. I was told the younger pediatric oncology patients usually received the Broviac. Teenagers, on the other hand, typically preferred the portecath, and the pain of accessing it, since it meant they could still wear a tank top in the midst of summer. Last year, my portecath had been removed with the hopes of never needing one again. This time, since the drugs were going to be so powerful, I had no choice. The broviac was necessary. But I was different now. I wasn't so worried about my appearance. I knew I was going to lose my hair and, unlike last time, I was not undressing for PE class worrying that someone would see my catheter. I wouldn't return to college until my treatments were completed. That is, if I survived. And just like that, the cancer tornado blew in and turned my world back upside down.

I woke up in the recovery room and immediately looked down. I expected the two-prong catheter to be dangling from my chest, but when my eyes reached their focal point, there was only a small bandage in its place. My heart started to race. *What is going on?* I was still groggy from the anesthesia but I was sobering up real quick. My mother was sitting in the chair beside my bed. "Mom, what's going on?" I asked. I could tell she didn't know what to say. She needed to tell me the truth but like so many other times in her life, she just wanted to protect me. She looked at me but remained silent. "Mom! Where's the Broviac?" I yelled. She told me that they didn't put it in. During the biopsy, they rushed the sample extracted from my chest down to the lab where an initial test was processed while I remained open on the table. The results were negative for malignancy. The next day Dr. D came into my hospital room. He proceeded to speak the best three words I have ever heard in my entire life: "It's scar tissue." *Wait? What? I don't have cancer? It didn't come back? My body hasn't betrayed me?*

Prepared to spend the next year under my covers in my mother's home trying to hold onto my sanity, I was now being told that I would recover from surgery within days and could return to school as scheduled. In five days. *Deep breath. Deep breath. Is someone playing a sick, sick, joke on me?* That day I learned, loud and clear, that my history would never truly be history. Hodgkin's would always be part of my life, but what exactly did that mean, and where would I go from here?

Five days later I packed up my car as originally planned and drove to Rutgers. I walked into the sorority house and felt like the past two weeks had been a bad dream. Everyone was jumping and laughing and hugging in the family room. I was back in the world I wanted to live in, the world that would have come so naturally to me if cancer had never entered my life. But instead of enjoying the homecoming, I was once again reminded of my mortality. I felt estranged from this world. *Where the hell do I belong?* I wanted to cry. I wanted to scream. I was grateful to be alive. I was angry that I had the issues of a seventy-five-year-old. There wasn't a peer in sight who could relate to me. I didn't feel validated, and I sure as hell didn't feel normal. Would I ever heal? I wanted to tell someone about the past week and the crazy thoughts running through my head like, "Can you believe that doctor? He didn't even apologize for scaring the shit out of me?" or "I was really scared. I am really scared. I don't want to die." But that didn't happen. I didn't even tell Karen. I didn't want to solidify the fact that I was indeed, different. I wish I could have taken the leap of faith and believed in my friends. I just wanted to talk and have someone listen. But I was too scared of seeing the fear in their eyes, so I didn't jump. When I looked in the mirror, I wanted to see the sixteen-year-old girl in the pictures I had taped all over my walls. But instead, a nineteen-year-old stranger stared me down. Who was this mysterious new girl that felt like a stranger in my body? My worlds became even more polarized, and I needed relief.

Like a crusader searching through the desert, I was on a mission to find that lost girl. Unfortunately, this unstoppable journey lent itself to an injurious and obsessive cycle of self-loathing. I turned to alcohol to get me through each day. After a few sips of cranberry and vodka, or Malibu rum and pineapple juice, I felt like the girl I wanted to be. By the time I hit the bar in the evening, I was dancing and singing with my friends and life seemed simple again. For a few hours, I would experience the sense of freedom and confidence that I used to feel. But when the sun came up, I was scared and alienated from myself once again. *Maybe the doctor was wrong—maybe the cancer is back? Maybe it isn't scar tissue?* I had to stop thinking those thoughts. And down went another shot.

Chapter 9
Bottom of the Bottle

I T WAS THE SATURDAY night of the Alpha Beta–Sigma Delta 80s mixer, and we were all wearing jeans and neon fringe T-shirts with turquoise-blue eye shadow. I decided to organize a cocktail hour in our room before leaving to meet the crowd at the fraternity house. I mixed up some insanely strong margaritas. Gigi said, "Deb, that's a glass of tequila with a splash of mix! You aren't going to remember half the night if you keep going at that pace." *Isn't that the point?* Although the name of the mixer changed—Masquerade mixer, Luau night, or Reggae Rumble—the evening repeated itself over and over and over again. The alcohol helped convince me that I was funny, attractive, or just worth talking to. And then the morning repeated itself. I awoke sweaty and nauseated, still working the previous night's round of shots out of my system and in desperate need of a toasted bagel and lemon lime Gatorade. After breakfast, the inevitable self-loathing began. *I'm empty. I'm disgusting. And, not to mention, revolting to look at.* But all it took was a quick shot of liquid courage to get me out of bed. In moments, the layers of shame and ugliness began to dissipate. I couldn't stop.

As the months passed, it took more and more red solo cups to make me feel like I belonged in my body. I knew I was out of control, but had no idea how to fix it. My gut told me that I needed help but I didn't know where to turn. My friends from high school were off at different colleges living new lives. My college friends had no clue about my history. Karen and I had grown apart. My family was just so damn happy that I survived the treatments that it never dawned on them to ask how I was doing emotionally. Old friends would drop lines like "You must feel so lucky" or "Forget that it even happened and go back to your normal life." My mind agreed but my soul was in anarchy. I was utterly alone.

On a Tuesday morning in mid-December, in the midst of final exams, I woke up in the bathroom of our sorority house. As I peeled my cheek from the toilet seat, I scanned my body. My shirt was ripped, skirt stained, and one of my black leather heels was floating inside the toilet amidst my vomit. And my nails, horrifically, were broken, chipped, and colorless. It had been months since I broke out my nail kit and they were staring up at me saying, "Why are you doing this? Why aren't you taking care of us?" I remembered during chemo when I would apply a coat of Cotton Candy and the purest of pinks would bring my mood to a wonderful place. Now not even Cotton Candy or any of her sisters could save me. It seemed useless to beautify my outside when

I felt so ugly on the inside. I smelled like smoke, body odor, hairspray, cranberry juice, beer, and French fries. *How did this happen? I don't want to give up.* Desperate to save myself, I secretly researched psychotherapists in the area surrounding campus. *I need to talk to someone.* I couldn't go on with everything all bottled up. I was too afraid to go to the student counseling center on the off chance that someone might see me. So I called a random doctor in the yellow pages, asked if I could come in for a free consultation, and arrived at his office a few days later. I'd never been to a therapist before. The only one I knew was Dr. W, and he offered me pie! This guy didn't look like he was about to offer me pie.

After cordial introductions, I sat down on the chair across from him. He asked several formal questions, and I answered. First, he asked if I was thinking of harming myself or others. After recovering from the shock of his candor, I truthfully responded, "Absolutely not."

Then he asked, "Why are you here today, Deborah?"

I froze. How could I explain to this guy that I'd lived through darkness but didn't really survive? I couldn't open up. I was scared. Taking a serious Freudian approach, he stared at me, waiting. *How do I tell him— I'm lost. I'm in pain. I've lost my beauty. I've lost my sobriety. I've lost my body. I've lost my confidence and my sense of self. I can't live like this. This isn't living. How do I go on?* He continued to stare at me in silence. I shut down. Maybe if we'd had three days a week of analysis on the couch, this would have eventually created a dynamic where I would feel safe enough to confide in him. But we were strangers. He was providing a mirror, and I didn't want to see my reflection. I had avoided myself for over two years and I wasn't about to take my first look with a total stranger staring back at me. We spent most of the hour in silence, and then I left.

I headed straight for the sorority house, swerved into my parking space, ran to my room, grabbed the travel bottles of rum from under my bed and swigged them down—one after another. *What is wrong with me?* I interpreted the psychiatrist's silence to mean, "Why are you here? Nothing is wrong with you. You are healthy, aren't you?" By the time three or four empty bottles collected on the floor, I felt like myself again. I pulled it together and headed to the library to meet up with my classmates to work on a group project in Food and Nutrition 101. Oh the irony. I continued to exist.

When I walked into my dorm room on the first day as a freshman, I was 5'4" tall and 110 pounds. Three years later, weeks before the end of my Junior year, my body had morphed into a reflection of my self image: unattractive, broken, and lost. I was up around 150 pounds. My legs jiggled, my arms jiggled—I even felt like my ankles jiggled. My skin was doughy and pimply since I was usually too inebriated to wash off the caked on make-up that I applied before leaving for the bar. Couple that with the pizza oil all over my fingertips which were screaming for a good soak in bubbly water and some cuticle care. I couldn't think, I obviously couldn't study, and I didn't want to feel. I couldn't remember being happy. I had confused drunkenness for joy. I had spent the last three years using alcohol to mask my feelings of inadequacy, but it never quite filled the void. It just made me forget it was there. I didn't know how to grow or mourn or fill the gaps.

I sat in my room, amidst a landscape of empty Hershey bar wrappers and mini vodka bottles, while the tears streamed down my face. *Who am I? I'm not the girl I once was. I certainly am not the girl I want to be. I'm not even the girl I'm pretending to be.* I cried, knowing that I had to make the phone call I'd been dreading. The message I never wanted my mother to hear. *How can I tell her, after all she's done for me, and all she sacrificed to save me, that I don't know how to live? I don't know how to be happy. Being alive isn't enough.* I picked up the phone and dialed.

I was sobbing. My mom couldn't understand a word that I said. "I need to come home. I'm dropping out of school. I can't do this anymore."

Shocked, my mother said, "Deb, what's going on? Tell me, what's wrong?" There was no quick answer. I didn't even know myself. The whole point was that I needed to figure it out. Depression had consumed me and I could barely see. I felt guilty, which only exacerbated the issue. I just kept saying, "I need to come home. I can't be here."

I pulled into my driveway the following day. My mother was waiting on the porch. I got out of the car and she wrapped her arms around me. She just held me and it felt wonderful. From sixteen to twenty years old I tried to digest my issues of mortality alone. It just wasn't natural, and obviously the weight of my silence crushed me. I didn't understand depression, and I certainly didn't appreciate the need to process a traumatic illness. I had been flying solo and had led myself down all the wrong roads. But I'd come home and was determined to find someone who could help me.

As much as my mother wanted to ease my pain, I couldn't talk to her about what was going on. It was like asking someone who is deathly afraid of heights to take skydiving lessons with you. I remembered her face during every medical meeting, every treatment, every needle stick, and every fever. She muscled through, but it looked like she was going to vomit every day. I wasn't going to dump my internal darkness onto my mother.

The next morning my mom and I returned to the medical center—my home away from home. I knew the corridors like I knew the freckles on my nose. We turned right, and then left. We passed the hall that led to the infusion suite where the kids were lined up like sardines, hoping that the liquid in their IVs would kick the shit out the cancer cells invading their bodies. I stopped dead in my tracks. I was not an active patient. I didn't belong in the infusion suite anymore, yet I ached to return. I guess being one of those sardines made me feel a little less alone. I didn't realize the power of being surrounded by other kids who woke up each morning and felt just as scared, just as nauseated, and looked just as bald as I did. Tears and screams were common in these hallways and empathy, not sympathy, poured out like champagne on New Year's Eve. In those halls, I never needed to walk with my eyes towards the floor or apologize for the way I looked. I wasn't embarrassed if there was a bloodstain on my shirt. I missed that freedom and acceptance.

At the door to the infusion clinic, my mother stopped me and said, "No, Deb, not that way. In here." She pointed her finger down an adjacent hallway. I was fully aware of where we were going, but my legs didn't want to listen to my brain. With enormous effort, I made an about face and walked to Dr. W's office.

During my treatment, months after the initial shock of the diagnosis, I was encouraged to speak to Dr. W about my transition from teenage girl to patient. In those sessions, I was usually upbeat and positive. I was too busy trying to pass French and AP English, filling out college applications, and focusing on my treatments to start dissecting the inner workings of my psyche. I was too busy trying not to lose my fucking mind. There was clearly no room for reflection. But now, four years later, I realized that may not have been the best game plan.

When I walked into Dr. W's office, he turned to me, smiled and said, "Hey girl, I've been waiting for you." Before my butt hit the chair, tears were running down my face. He knew. He was a smart man. He knew that once I started trying to live again, I would ultimately have to feel again. And what I felt was fear. Constantly. I was supposed to focus on math, science, art, and history. I was supposed to be interested in boys, make-up, and clothes. But when I closed my eyes at night, my fingers grazed the scars on my chest and I shivered from the fear that one day the Hodgkin's would be back.

I continued to sit next to Dr. W and cry, probably for two or three sessions. I cried, cried, and cried. I wasn't crying about boy issues or the love handles that had taken up residence over the top of my jeans. I cried because I was terrified. I'd been scared for years and hadn't expressed any of it. The fear that was so ridiculously appropriate needed to come out.

Finally, a few sessions in, Dr. W started to speak. "Wow—that was a lot of crying," he remarked. I laughed. "So, do *you* know why you're here?" he asked.

I replied, "I think so. I came here because I need a life raft. You give those out, right?"

We giggled. I asked, "Am I crazy Dr. W?"

"No, you are not crazy, Deb," he said. He took the next several minutes to describe to me, in detail, what my body and mind had gone through and how the physical and emotional were connected. He talked about each treatment cycle, each medication, every side effect, the social hurdles that paralleled those years, the surgeries, the scars, the scare two years ago and the ever present mortality cloud that hovered over anyone in my position. We looked into each other's eyes and digested the gravity of that moment.

I cried some more. I asked him why I couldn't just move on with my life. Why did I have to relive this? I asked, "Aren't I supposed to just get back on the horse?"

"No, my dear. Cancer bulldozed its way into your life—a bomb went off inside of you, and you're left with a pile of rubble. It's been three years since your last treatment, but you're still a big heap of disaster. You're supposed to be totally freaked out. You're supposed to cry and punch and push and yell and think that you're going to die from the sadness and fear that consumes you. And then afterwards, once the tears subside, you'll accept your past, and we, together, will find all of your pieces and put them together again, and you'll be ready to move forward. I promise, Deb. You will."

I exhaled for the first time in years. We spent many days talking and crying. I released my soul-crushing fears into the air and he caught them. They weren't mine alone anymore. I had a partner who validated what I was feeling.

It was our fourth session and Dr. W pulled out a mirror. "What do you see?" he asked.

"I see a girl who doesn't fit into her Levi's," I said. "I see a girl who is different. I see a girl who is sad she has fought so hard to live and now doesn't know how."

"What do you dream of seeing?" he asked.

"I dream of seeing that girl from April 28th…four years ago." I cried.

"I know you do. And part of her is sitting right here. And part of her is gone. But there's also the part of you that you don't even know yet. Yes, cancer took something from you but I'm going to show you what it gave you. Besides depression, that is."

So, just pressing the pause button for a moment—taking the time to work through my thoughts with Dr. W—sparked a new beginning. We talked and talked and talked. He validated and validated and validated. I slowly started to believe in myself again. I believed in my existence. One day he asked, "Who are you?" I responded like a fourth-grader: "I love chocolate. I love the color purple. I love my family. I love my friends. I love the smell of honeysuckle." That night I busted out my nail kit—Pinking up the Pieces for both fingers and toes.

One day, Dr. W asked, "Do you remember the pie?"

I responded, with faux annoyance, "Of course I remember the pie, you crazy man."

He laughed and then we talked about a little word called *denial*. Denial—"the refusal to admit the truth or reality." *Damn straight*. My denial began seconds after taking my first steps through the medical center doors. Within minutes of hearing the words *cancer, Hodgkins,* and *chemotherapy*, my defenses grew stronger. On one hand, denial was my hero, gallantly showing up at my doorstep, as if on a white horse with a lance in hand, ready to kick some ass. Denial's power allowed me to digest information at my own pace. In turn, I was able to get up, shower, and put one foot in front of the other. My typical prompt self did not rush out of the house to make our 9:00 a.m. appointment that first morning, nor did I catch on when I read the words "pediatric oncology" on the plaque beside the elevator, and the arrow pointed straight towards my hospital room. Denial kept my body in that bed and prevented me from running out the door with my arms flailing up and down. The protective dam that only allowed certain bits and pieces to come through enabled me to sit and listen. I probably heard one out of every twenty words that were spoken, but that's what needed to happen. Maybe that was the secret of the pie. I couldn't possibly absorb all that was going on physically, emotionally, and mentally in that moment. It was too much. The only way to get through it was to face one needle, one surgery, one chemo, one moment at a time.

When I graduated from high school and was sent back into the world to begin my life again, denial stayed glued to my side. Given everyone's excited expectation, I tried to move on and just be happy. But something wasn't right. I had learned how to fight for my life, how to survive. And then I had to just sit and wait? There were no more treatments, no more pills, no more radiation. There was no more fighting. There was nothing to actually do for three months until my next scans either came back clean, or not. The inaction was impossible for me.

Dr. W helped me dissect the transition from patient back to young woman. I had to process this trauma at my own pace, but couldn't there have been an easier way? I'd withstood my share of embarrassing drunk moments.

I'd braved suffocation from the stretched out, ripped jeans that barely made it over my thunder thighs. Dr. W knew I had been persevering, trying to camouflage my years of treatment like they never happened. But they existed, and whether I liked it or not, cancer was now a big part of who I was—past, present, and future. Without owning that, I was living as an imposter. I was punishing myself with every drink and candy bar and I was hurting everyone around me at the same time. I was confused and utterly embarrassed to admit that I was anything but thankful and joyous. I wanted to be the good daughter, the good friend, and the good patient. I should have been grateful as hell to even be alive. What did I have to complain about? I'd won the war, right? That's what my scans said. The road back to normal—the new normal that is—was so complicated. There were so many crossroads, and each presented me with an opportunity to make a bad decision.

During my summer with Dr. W, I learned how the mind and body heal and how I could help myself through the process. I learned the importance of giving myself a break and taking the time I needed. From soaking in a bubble bath and crying, to writing in a journal or attending a support group, the validation of my sadness and fear redirected me towards stability. I had been terrified that returning to those dark places would bring me deeper into the abyss of self-hatred, so I'd fought against the urge to explore them. Dr. W taught me that the urge to explore the dark was really the pathway back into the light. It was the force telling me that I needed to recover before I could move forward. Dwell, dwell, dwell—it's how we heal. So I cut myself some slack and set aside time to readjust to this new world. After repeatedly asking myself who I was and what defined me, I finally found a starting point. I was a fighter—some said a survivor. But I didn't feel safe without the fight because the fight was how I survived. So the road to rediscovering myself was a continuous process that I worked on every day. As time elapsed, it got easier.

On a mild summer Tuesday, after writing in my journal and adding a coat of E-nuff is E-nuff to my toes, I walked over to my bedroom closet. I took a deep breath, and with a huge lump in the back of my throat I opened the door. I reached towards the back wall where it had been living for over four years. With all my strength, I grabbed the long, brown, curly haired monster that haunted me. "This is over!" I ran downstairs and threw the wig in the kitchen garbage. *Not good enough*. I pulled the trash out of the pail and closed it up with a twisty tie. Instead of dropping it in the garbage can in our garage, I walked down the street to the park, barefoot, mind you, because my toes were still drying, and threw it into the garbage beside the swing set. I walked home, went straight upstairs, and lay down on my plush lavender carpet. Exhale… *I'm making progress*. I felt stronger. Freer. I looked back into my closet where the animal no longer resided and pulled out my running sneakers.

Dust had settled on the laces. Wondering if they would still fit, I slipped them on—only after checking to make sure my toes were dry. Like Cinderella's slippers, they cushioned my feet perfectly. From that day on, I began to run. As the weeks passed, the pounds melted away. Glimmers of light began to shine again. My summer of therapy didn't extinguish my fear of death or suddenly turn me back into the girl I was before cancer, but it gave me the confidence to rebuild. There was no flip-the-switch moment. On the contrary, finding myself again was a slow and arduous process. But I had taken the first steps.

By the time fall rolled in, I was ready to start my senior year. I felt like a tadpole learning how to swim. I knew it would take time for me to grow into a person ready to accept—and to believe in—myself again. But I had undergone a rebirth and slowly, very slowly, I started to trust the foundation of my new identity. It was time to open my eyes and confront what I'd seen in the mirror. I had to embrace my body, scars and all. I'd found a new color to help. So with a shiny fresh coat of Naked Truth on my fingers and toes, I drove back to campus and headed straight to the sorority house.

Some of the girls were sitting on the steps talking and laughing. They were my younger sisters and were excited to start their sophomore year. They stopped when they saw me, asked for some advice on selecting classes, professors, etc. It felt good to be able to offer some advice. I noticed Stacy holding a bottle of

Luscious Lilac and I smiled. Girls will be girls. I walked back to my car and began to haul the clothes, linens, pillows, books, shoes and everything else a collegiate girl needs to survive, up to my room on the third floor. Months ago, I had fled this room in hysterics, thinking I would never get back to solid ground. I took slow, deep breaths and started to unpack. I assembled the layers of my bedding, which always made me feel cozy and safe. First my sheets, then my comforter, pillowcases, shams, and finally some decorative pillows to complete the look. I reached into the bottom of my bag to make sure I hadn't missed anything. I panicked for a moment. *Is there something dead in here?* But as I pulled out my old friend, I welled up with tears. These were new tears, representing relief, growth, and reflection. Bear had come to college. My mother must have snuck him into my bag before I left. As I placed him in the middle of all my pillows, I could hear her say, "Wherever you are, I am right next door. I love you."

Shortly thereafter, my girls barged through the door screaming and smiling. They threw me onto the ground with hugs. Months felt like decades, and we were all so glad to be back together. It felt good to be present. We sat on my bed and talked about our summers. I opened up. I told them about my sessions with Dr. W and how I did a lot of crying and ran two miles, and cried more, and ran four miles. Trish asked, "Shit Deb, why didn't you talk to us?" "I just couldn't," I responded. And then Gigi said, "You look beautiful." She wasn't talking about my sleek toned legs, but rather the inner peace I had finally found. More tears fell.

In high school, no one was able to stand in those dark spaces with me. It made people uncomfortable when I talked about my health. That shit was so scary. It was totally understandable. But I'd become so guarded, so used to dealing with the emotion on my own, that when my girlfriends offered up honest support, something changed. I'd attended a few support groups over the summer and spoken to survivors as well, but there's something about a girlfriend—a giggle till you pee in your pants kind of girlfriend—that provides a different sense of connection. The strength, which is carried in a true friendship, is invisible but undeniably great. Sitting on my bed with my friends, I realized with certainty that I'd been doing this all wrong. I'd been pushing away the support that had been there the whole time. Instead of protecting them (and me), I began to discuss moments that I knew they could handle. It just so happened that my girlfriends could actually tolerate gore—the messy, disgusting, bloody, part of the story. Who knew? They had each experienced their share of skinned knees and broken arms. They knew gross and could relate on their own level. It was an amazing start.

Chapter 10
Turks & Caicos

AFTER GRADUATING FROM RUTGERS with a B.S. in marketing, I moved to New York City with a newfound confidence and strength. No longer pudgy and lost, I stood a lean 120 pounds and was finally in control of my body—and my life. My hair grew back to its long, curly state, and I decided it was a marvelous idea to start off my professional life as blonde. I was now an adult, or at least that's what people were calling me as I entered the "real world."

I moved into my first apartment, 205 East 95th on Manhattan's Upper East Side, and was exploding with excitement. I parked the U-Haul on the corner of 3rd Avenue, and hauled my stuff with the help of my brother's brawn. Vicki, one of my two new roommates, opened the door. She was a family friend who I didn't know very well at the time, but it was obvious she was kind and genuine. My other roommate, Kim, was a ball of fire, running from room to room getting ready for Friday night's festivities while yelling from the bathroom, "Nice to meet you!" *My first apartment. Amazing.*

Vicki and I both worked at public relations firms, and Kim was a cardiac nurse at a local hospital. We worked hard all week, but when Friday night rolled in we let loose. Ever aware of my self-medicating past, I carefully enjoyed the bar scene and nightlife in the Big Apple. Occasionally, I would meet a cute guy at a bar or club. Even though I had made much progress, I was still so damn scared of opening up to someone. I had this core-crushing fear that my past would keep me imprisoned and that I would never fall in love. I was even more terrified that I'd meet the man of my dreams but that he wouldn't fall in love with me, sure that as soon as cancer hit the airwaves, he would turn and run. On top of that, my twelve-year-old self, the one that was left alone in her sleeping bag while Jennie Cohen was getting felt up a few feet away, still reminded me that love was conditional and could disappear if I didn't measure up. To add flame to the fire, my gynecologist, Dr. H, would say, "You know your treatment did a number on your eggs, and they aren't getting any younger!" *Great.*

After three years of my new city life, grinding through my weekly routine of writing press releases and organizing events Monday through Friday, I was losing steam. Sitting at my desk staring at my to-do list, the energy to push through my daily grind as an underpaid publicist dissipated. I tried to look out the window and take in the change of season, but my cubicle was windowless. I leaned back in my chair to see through to my boss's office window. I kept leaning. Boom—I hit the floor. *I hate this cubicle.*

Maybe the end of summer sparked something inside me. Maybe it reminded me of what it felt like to be excited about something new. Fall was a time for beginnings and new challenges, but my work life didn't measure up anymore. But what did I want to do? What should I devote my life to? I had no idea.

On a Tuesday morning in September, I was walking to my office from the 14th Street subway station. As I made the left turn onto Fifth Avenue I noticed everyone looking up in the sky. I gaped at the fire and smoke coming out of one of the Twin Towers. Like many others, I couldn't digest the gravity of that moment, and I walked quickly into my office building on Twelfth Street and took the elevator up. When the doors opened on the 11th floor, I saw my colleagues gathered by the south-facing floor-to-ceiling windows of the loft. *Oh my God.* I watched with confusion. Suddenly, the second tower seemed to explode before my eyes. I immediately called my parents and my brother but could not get through. My boss said, "Everyone just go back to your desks. It's okay." *What, you crazy bitch?!* We listened on the radio trying to process the words "terrorist attack." Then the unimaginable happened. We watched with horror as the first tower plummeted to the ground. "No!" I screamed and threw my hands against the glass. I needed to go home. I needed to be with my friends and family. I needed to not be here. And then the second tower fell. As I walked home, up 3rd Avenue, with hundreds of other New Yorkers, breathing the smoke-filled air, I felt an irresistible urge to be of help to someone.

Weeks passed as New Yorkers and the world came together to mourn those lost on September 11th. It was a day that pierced our humanity. I called agencies, relief organizations, and shelters to see if I could assist in any way. I was usually told, "Thank you for calling, but we have enough help right now." But some organizations asked, "Are you a social worker or counselor?" And I would reply, "No, I'm in PR and marketing." I thought about Dr. W and how that kind of connection with someone changed my life. I thought about his ability to sit with me on those dark days, and I knew he didn't want to be anywhere else. He didn't feel uncomfortable. He wasn't at a loss for words. He didn't pity me. He didn't tell me to just get back on the horse. He told me I wasn't crazy. *Maybe I can do that for someone else. Maybe I can be the asshole who offers someone pie.*

Several weeks later I found myself sitting on my bedroom floor with five different applications for social work programs all around the city. Kim was banging on my door asking when I would be ready to help highlight her hair. "I'll be right there! Hold on!" I yelled through the door. I eagerly began to fill out each one. *I want to do this. I really want to do this.*

"Deb! C'mon!" Kim yelled.

"Okay, okay— I'm here," I said as I opened the door.

"What were you doing in there?" she asked.

"Just figuring out my life," I giggled.

"I hear ya," she said.

Within a few weeks, my applications were completed and in the mail. I just had to wait and see. I was sitting at my desk, trying to concentrate on the job that still paid the bills, when my friend Gigi called on my office line. "Hey, girl. Get your passport ready, we're planning a trip. Let's go somewhere with white sand, turquoise water and pink drinks with paper umbrellas."

"Yes!" I cried. It was perfect timing. We weren't going to get on the plane for two more months, but the mere dream of sitting on a beach and letting the sun soak in kept me plugging through my assignment—the all-important launch of Razzberry Pop Treats.

Two days before our flight I got a package in the mail from Yeshiva University, my first choice. *Oh my God, it's so thick. Oh my God.* I ripped open the envelope as quickly as possible and read, "Dear Deborah, Congratulations…" "Yes! Yes! Yes!" I screamed out loud and began jumping up and down in the middle of the living room. I called my parents and reported the news with pride. It felt so right.

With new direction and in much need of a tan, four of us flew down to Club Med Turks and Caicos. On our second night at the resort, dressed in a fuchsia halter top and white shorts, I sat at the bar and ordered my second Jack and Diet Coke—I'd finally learned how to sip and enjoy a cocktail. As I bopped my head to J. Lo's "Play," I looked over and saw Sarah talking with two guys. My gaze instantly fell on one of them. He was tall and lean, with a swimmer's body, brown hair, and green eyes. Just adorable. I grabbed my plastic cup and sauntered over to introduce myself. They were brothers from New York. *What a cutie-pie!* I tried my best to flirt in a not-so-obvious way.

Before I knew it, Andrew and I were on the dance floor and our bodies grooved together until the bar closed. Not wanting the night to end, we walked over to the pool and sat down, dangling our legs in the water. "Hey, what happened?" he asked. "What are those scars on your chest?"

Okay, Deb, you can do this. Just tell him. I liked this guy and I was going to put it all out there for the very first time in my life. *I'm in the Caribbean. If there's ever a time to test this method, the truth method, it's now. You haven't fallen in love with this guy. He can't break your heart tonight. Just do it.* And so I opened up. I told Andrew that I was diagnosed with cancer when I was sixteen-years-old and that I underwent several rounds of chemotherapy and radiation. The scars were from the biopsies and the surgeries. Expecting the typical wide-eyed frightened look, and uncomfortable silence from the other party, I was taken by surprise. He continued to stare at my face and kick his legs in the water, intertwining mine. He didn't react. It was like I just told him my favorite ice cream flavor was mint chocolate chip. No pity, no shock, no uncomfortable silence. And he didn't run away. After hanging by the pool for a few more hours and getting to know one another, we realized that the sun was close to rising. Andrew walked me back to my room, gently wrapped his arms around my waist and kissed me goodnight. I had heard myths about seeing fireworks when true love strikes, but I had never experienced such a dramatic reaction to a kiss. When Andrew's lips touched mine for the first time it took every ounce of strength I had to stay afloat. My knees turned to Jell-O and my mind went blank. *What just happened?* We spent the next few days flirting, snorkeling, and dancing. I was sad when the time came to return to the real world. As my girlfriends and I waited in the resort lobby for a cab to bring us to the airport, Andrew sat beside me. He took my phone and plugged in his number. We kissed goodbye, for now.

A few weeks later, back in New York, Andrew and I went on our first official date. He rang the doorbell of my 500-square-foot, two-bedroom walk-up apartment on 23rd Street and 3rd Avenue. I answered the door, saw his smiling face and couldn't help but giggle. We sat on the couch, caught up, kissed, laughed, and began our adventure as a couple. Andrew was a junior at Columbia and was five years younger than I was. At first, my friends couldn't believe I was dating such a youngin' and they teased me about robbing the cradle. But eventually they realized what I had known since day one. He was the kindest, most generous, loving soul I had ever met. A decade after cancer imprinted its stamp on me, a very special man inspired me to believe again. Timber... I'm falling in love.

Like every other twenty-something in New York City, Andrew and I both played musical apartments, searching for a few more square feet without spending 80% of our paychecks. I moved from East 23rd Street to West 65th Street to be closer to grad school. He moved from West 120th Street to East 31st Street when he graduated from Columbia.

We took the subway back and forth a few times a week to spend time together. Andrew didn't fancy going to the latest restaurant or nightclubs, so we strolled through Central Park and shared a popsicle, or found a local street fair and bought twenty pairs of socks for two dollars. We usually ended up snuggled in bed watching *Law & Order* reruns and munching on sushi delivery. It was perfect. When I needed a girlfriend fix, I met my gals for mani-pedis, dinner, and cocktails.

On June 14, 2003, my 27th birthday, Andrew took me out for Japanese and toasted to a great upcoming summer. He reached into his workbag and pulled out an envelope. It wasn't a beautifully wrapped box adorned with ribbon, but I knew it was my present. *What did he get me?* He handed me the envelope and I smiled nervously as I opened it. A brochure for a two-week pottery workshop? Although Andrew was an engineer by trade, he was also an amazing artist. He'd been working with clay since he was fourteen and thought this could be a fun escapade for us to share. The brochure described world-renowned instructors, delicious meals served between lessons on the wheel, a beautiful atmosphere, and wait—where was this place? In freakin' Tuscany, Italy? It was so Andrew. No frills, no extravagant build up, no fancy box, but romantic as hell. We spent an incredible three weeks together, eating our way through Tuscany, Florence, and Siena. I'd found my forever.

My life was in balance. I'd come a long way.

Chapter 11
Buckle Up Baby

TIME FLIES WHEN YOU'RE happy, busy, and in love. Andrew and I had been together for three years. I graduated from my masters program and started my first job as a social worker. It was invigorating to finally get my head out of the books and begin working again. After seeing twenty or thirty patients a day, organizing treatment plans and team meetings, I'd meet Andrew for dinner or gather with friends to watch *Sex and the City*. Life was pretty normal. But just when you think you have it all figured out, *boom*.

We drove up to the Catskills on a Friday night in February. Six of us piled into our station wagon and looked forward to a weekend out of Manhattan. After enjoying a country breakfast of eggs, pancakes, and half coffee/half hot chocolate, we were off to the slopes. The conditions were perfect, including a fresh coat of powder on the mountain. While my bindings were adjusted, Andrew asked, "Are you going to try Challenger today or what?"

"Or what." I replied.

"C'mon babe. Try it!"

"I *could* try it. I also *could* die." He relentlessly continued. "We'll decide when we get to the top of the mountain." "Yeah…that's when I'll change my mind—when I'm staring down 2,000 feet."

I'd been running pretty regularly and felt strong. Unlike Andrew, who loved to rip down the mountain on his snowboard, my style was more slow and steady. Keeping my skis in the pizza pie position, I glided leisurely down the slope as Andrew and our friends whisked by me. I took in the snow-covered peaks and inhaled the cold air into my lungs. Sunday night came quickly and we packed up our gear for the three hour ride back home. I reached toward the dashboard, pressed the seat warmer button, grabbed my bag and ran into the lodge. "I just need a second! Girl stuff," I yelled to Andrew across the parking lot. To my surprise, the extra super I had put it only two hours earlier was about to burst. *What is going on here?* I reached into the side pocket of my bag and grabbed another tampon. *Okay, I'll be fine for the ride home.* Still shivering from the mountain, I layered back up and headed to the car. "Ok, I'm here. I'm here. Let's go."

We were probably ten minutes away from my apartment when I felt wet. *Oh my God. Am I leaking?* We reached my front steps and I gave Andrew a huge kiss. "I had so much fun, honey. I love you," I said with my whole heart.

"I love you, babe. I'll call you tomorrow."

I walked up the four flights of stairs and unlocked the door. As I took off my clothes, it was clear that I had indeed leaked. *Holy crap.* I'd completely soaked through the tampon, my underwear, leggings, and ski pants. *Oh no—is there blood on Andrew's car seat?!* I rinsed my clothes in the sink, jumped in the shower, and happily climbed into bed.

The next morning I awoke, and thank goodness, my sheets were clean. But when I made my way to the bathroom, gravity said good morning. Blood dripped down my legs. I quickly grabbed a handful of toilet paper. *This is crazy.* Honestly nervous to go to work without a diaper, I called and left a message for my gynecologist. I had to get to work. By noon, after going to the bathroom every thirty minutes to check the status of my underwear, Dr. H called me back. "Dr. H, I got my period on Friday, as expected, but my flow is crazy. I'm going through a super tampon every hour or so. It's really, really heavy," I explained.

"Okay, well your hormones might be fluctuating for some reason. Why don't you double up on your birth control pill? It will probably resolve itself with a little extra estrogen. Call me in a few days."

That night, I returned home from work and decided to skip my run. I imagined my uterus bouncing up and down, and with every lunge forward on the treadmill, my vagina expelling a liter of blood. I opted for TV and a mani-pedi with the fresh bottle of Love & Acceptance I'd picked up last week. When my nails were completely dry, I took a long shower to rinse off the grimy period feeling. While deeply inhaling the calming scent of my peaches and cream shower gel, I noticed an enormous bruise above my left knee. *What the heck is this? I didn't fall once on the mountain.* Curious, I inspected my body further and found what looked like razor burn on my shins. It didn't seem to fit. I had just purchased new razor blades with the moisturizing tip and used more than enough pomegranate-scented shaving cream to avoid such a nuisance. *No swollen glands—check. High energy—check. No pain or fever check. No cancer. Could this be menopause? Do you lose your eggs in one big bloody flush?*

A few more days passed and I called Dr. H. "Hi, Deb. Have the pills helped?"

"No, I'm still very heavy. I had to buy the giant, nighttime Maxi Pads with wings that I haven't used since I was thirteen. I'm leaking through the super tampons, sometimes within an hour." After a few seconds of silence she said, "Okay, let's get some blood work done today and see what's going on. Where can I send the script?" *Blood work?* All of a sudden, the almost comical ski pant fiasco turned from annoying to something else. *What is happening? Is my body betraying me? Don't go there, Deb.*

I gave Dr. H the fax number to the lab downstairs in the hospital. I'd go as soon as I could, but first I needed to table my anxiety and get my ass to morning rounds. It was, like always, a busy day. I didn't arrive at the lab until after 5:00 p.m. The phlebotomist and I nodded to each other and she turned her attention to my arms. She spoke to my veins like they were kindergartners. "Let's see. Which one of you are we going to use? Oh, you look big and juicy." I shivered. It was a quick stick, three tubes filled, and then a sprint to catch the M6 that was about to pull away on 1st Avenue.

Although my flow was still ridiculously intense, I threw on my leggings, tank top, and sneakers and headed to the gym for a quick workout. As my feet pounded the treadmill, thoughts streamed in: *Deb, you are not sick. You are not sick.* I cranked the treadmill up to 7 mph. *See, you're fine. Maybe I'm having a miscarriage. Andrew and I use protection. Maybe my iron level is really low? Maybe I need to eat more spinach? Does spinach have iron?* I was grasping for something, anything, that didn't mean disaster. Before I knew it, an hour had passed and I was drenched with sweat. I felt strong. I thought I was healthy.

My calves ached the next morning as I slipped on my black pants and nude pumps. It was March 11th, 2005. I arrived at my desk clutching my customary half-caff latte, ready to start my day. A few minutes after 9:00 a.m., Dr. H's office called with my blood results. "We have your CBC results. Where are you?" *Where am I?* "I'm at work. Why?" "Please hold. Dr. H will be right with you."

I immediately knew I was in trouble. *Fuck!* She was scared for me, apprehensive, but tried to hide her concern.

"Hi, Deb. Your CBC came in and you have a critically low platelet count. You're at 4,000."

I was confused. "What? What does that mean?" "It's critically low. The normal range is between 160,000 and 450,000. I need you to go to your primary care doctor. Today. Now. Send me his fax number and I will send over your results."

I hung up the phone. *This is bad. I'm so confused. I feel fine.* I was spinning. *I have a critically low platelet count. What does that mean? More Hodgkin's? Please no cancer. Please no cancer.*

I blurted something incoherent to my supervisor, grabbed my coat, and ran out the door. I robotically hailed a cab to my Primary Care physician's office. I called Andrew and tried to calmly explain that something was wrong but I didn't really know what. "I'll meet you there," he stated with authority and hung up before I even said good-bye. I peered out the cab window and watched the pedestrians whizz by. I started to brace myself for medical disaster. *Please, God. Please let me be okay. I'll be a better person. I'll do whatever I need to do. I'm in love. My life is good. Please... I hope you're listening... If this can just be a minor problem, I'll be forever thankful.* As we turned onto Madison Avenue, I remembered the piping hot latte sitting on my desk. My gut said that something was terribly wrong and that delicious latte might have been the last sip of normalcy I'd taste for awhile.

I arrived at Dr. Primary Care's (PC) office, with a million thoughts racing through my head. *What does this symptom mean? Is my remission over? Have I appreciated the past ten years to their fullest? Am I going into surgery today? Am I starting chemotherapy? Is this just a huge mistake? Is Andrew going to leave me? Is this too much for him to handle? Deep breath, deep breath.*

Dr. PC met me in the exam room. "What's going on here?" he asked.

"You tell me. I'm kind of freaking out."

"First thing we are going to do is rerun the CBC." He took out a tourniquet, snapped it a few times, and stabbed my big vein. Minutes later he returned with my results. "It is 4,000. So, I believe you might have a condition called ITP—Idiopathic Thrombocytopenic Purpura. ITP is a blood disorder that can be cured relatively easily with a variety of medications."

It's not back. You're okay, Deb. It was all going to be okay. "We don't really know what triggers ITP. Your immune system is attacking the healthy platelets in your blood stream that your body needs for normal clotting. There is a spectrum of low platelet counts. Anything under 180,000 is considered low, so 4,000 is really low. At that level, you're at risk for spontaneous internal bleeding—it's not that big of a deal in your arm or leg, but if the bleed happens in your brain we have a problem."

"But I'm not in pain or anything. I ran six miles last night. I feel fine," I protested.

"You don't need to be in pain for something to be critically dangerous. I'm going to put in a call to my colleague over at Uptown Hospital. You'll have to be admitted immediately."

"Admitted? Now?" I asked in shock.

"With the risk of a spontaneous hemorrhage, you need to be seconds away from an operating room, not thirty minutes away at home." The fear dial cranked up. Just a few minutes ago Dr. PC's diagnosis of a treatable condition felt like a gift. Now, ITP seemed like a gun pointing at my head—one that could go off at any moment. I needed it cured. Immediately.

While Dr. PC called his colleague, Andrew burst through the door with his umbrella drawn like a sword, ready to attack the beast that was threatening the woman he loved. Unfortunately, his desire alone wasn't enough to protect me. I wrapped my arms around him and held on tight. I stared into his eyes and tried to communicate so many things to him in that instant. *One, don't freak out. Two, this is going to be a bumpy ride so get ready. Three, if you want to leave, I'll understand.*

We left the doctor's office with specific instructions to drive directly to the hospital where a team of white coats would be waiting for me. Talk about attention—and not the kind you want. I felt like the girl with the bad reputation. We stood on the street for a moment. We were bewildered—uprooted from our normal lives, unsure of where this would lead us. I turned to the left and then right. "Where's the car?" Andrew looked at me with hesitance. He wasn't sure if I'd be amused or infuriated. Andrew explained that he had driven like

Mario Andretti all the way from work to the doctor's office. In his state of crazed frustration, he double-parked the car in the middle of Park Avenue—and left his keys in the ignition. I laughed, grabbed his hand, and we sprinted as fast as our legs could carry us, hoping the car hadn't been towed away—almost forgetting the crisis surrounding us.

From the street, the hospital looked massive. I must have passed the gray brick building fifty times, but never wondered what was behind its façade. Andrew and I found the main entrance and walked quickly up the three stairs to the oversized automatic revolving door. There were signs everywhere directing patients to their destinations. We couldn't think straight, so our collective feet walked us directly to the information desk. "Where is Hematology?" I asked the ninety-two-year-old volunteer sitting behind the counter. "Good morning to you pretty lady. It's right over there on the first floor," he said pointing to the sign with an arrow directly in front of us. Andrew took my hand and we walked towards the door. "Good luck," the man called from behind me. I turned around and smiled. *Could he somehow see my history? Could he see my future? What's with these information desk people? Are they psychics?*

Day 1. There were three people in the Hematology waiting room. One was sleeping, slumped over in his chair, and two others were reading magazines. They were all between the ages of fifty and seventy-five. *I don't belong here.*

While we waited to be called, my senses heightened and the tension began to build. I heard machines beeping in the back room and printers churning out pathology reports. I smelled cleaning products—harsh hospital ones. It was vile. Triggered by the sounds and smells, I was sent back to the day I was diagnosed with Hodgkin's. Over a decade had passed, but it suddenly felt like yesterday. I recalled the powerlessness of being a patient and my stomach turned into an inferno. Cancer or not, I knew this was going to be a bumpy ride. I reached into my bag and dug out a peppermint candy. "Deborah, they're ready for you."

We were led back to the lab where phlebotomists were lined up like contestants in a dating game. They buzzed around their respective prey with precision and purpose, peeling labels and checking charts. "Over here at station four, sweetie." I looked around the blood room, and all eyes were on me. *What is she in here for? The same as me? Probably not. The guy over there looks pretty good. This chick on my right looks like shit. I hope I don't have what she has. She's probably thinking the same thing.* I stared at the empty glass vials on her tray with purple, yellow, and green tops all marked for analysis seeking different contaminants. *What are we looking for?* The nurse handled my arms like she was examining a melon at the grocery store. She poked and squeezed, looking for a vein that hadn't been abused. "Oh, that one looks really good," she muttered under her breath. "You've done this before I see," she noted as I pumped my fist to help the blood flow. I smirked. *Oh, if you only knew lady.* She inserted the needle and began to extract. A few seconds later she muttered again, "What's going on with this?"

"Is everything okay?" I asked, feeling like I was going to vomit.

"Yes, everything is fine," she responded as she adjusted the needle in my vein. I groaned. "Sorry, it was fine and then all of a sudden it stopped. Don't worry, I'll get it to work," she insisted.

"This is my third CBC in twenty-four hours and everyone has been using this vein so maybe it's just had enough," I explained.

"No, no—it's fine sweetie. Don't worry." *I'm not worried, I'm pissed. You're butchering my vein and it hurts. Please don't speak to me like I'm seven.*

After the blood draw, I was led to an exam room where I waited for the hematologist. It only took about five minutes for the centrifuge machine to generate my platelet count. The doctor walked in, smiled and introduced himself. "Hi, I'm Dr. R." He then confirmed for the third time that my platelet count was, indeed, critically low. Although I kept hearing the word "critical," no one seemed alarmed by this diagnosis, minus the talk of a spontaneous brain hemorrhage. "Deb, we think Dr. PC was right and that you have ITP. There is no test for ITP. It's diagnosed by ruling out more severe illnesses that have the same symptoms. It's sometimes caused by a virus and sometimes for no reason at all. However, given your history, I need to rule out a more serious condition. Have you ever had a bone-marrow biopsy?" I remembered those words. I never had to endure the test, but my comrades in the pediatric oncology suite did, and I remembered, clear as day, the screams that bellowed through the halls while the biopsies were performed.

"No Dr. R, I've never had one. Are you going to do one right now? On me?"

"Yes, we have to rule out more serious alternatives." *There's that word again. He doesn't want to say cancer, but I know that's what he's thinking.* I took a deep breath. There was nowhere to run. I looked at Andrew. I was terrified. *Shit! Shit! Shit!*

"This is going to hurt so badly, isn't it?" I asked with a nervous smile.

"Unfortunately, yes," he responded kindly. No time for drugs, no time to waste, I just had to do it. I'd already transformed from the lighthearted, career-driven woman who rode the crosstown bus to work into my alter ego, the patient. *How bad can it really be, right?*

"Andrew, we're going to Bloomingdales after this to buy a pair of chocolate brown suede boots." We laughed nervously because, well…what else could we do?

Moments later, I was lying on the exam table, my bare back and half my ass exposed, gripping Andrew's hand. Behind me, I heard Dr. R unwrapping and assembling the bone marrow extractor like he was putting together a rocket launcher. I gulped. I felt a cold alcohol swab run over my lower back, and then heard, "Hold on." When your doctor actually tells you to hold on, it's really going to hurt. He inserted the contraption.

"Holy shit! Fuck!" I felt every twist and turn as Dr. R cranked the drill into my hipbone like a corkscrew. My fingernails drew blood from Andrew's palm as tears streamed down my face. Dr. R used my back as leverage while he and the nurse turned the lever digging through the bone's exterior. *Please be over!* But the worst was yet to come. He used his little gizmo to pull out the chunk of bone he needed. Words cannot describe the pain. But then it was over. My face hit the pillow and I started to pant. *It's over, it's over, it's over.*

Andrew handed me a cup of water while the nurse applied a bandage with pressure. I wanted to regroup but when I got up and tried to button my jeans. In a wave of exhaustion, I dropped back down to the bed. *I'll just leave my pants open.* There was no need to pretend that I was some well mannered lady after yelling truck driver obscenities at the top of my lungs. I thought it was crazy that a mere Scooby Doo band-aid was the only evidence left of the procedure.

I was given a minute to compose myself before I was sent to my hospital room. The elevator doors opened and there it was, the sign Hematology & Oncology. *Ugh. Why do they need to be married?* It smelled like disinfectant covering up something even more putrid. *Maybe someone just vomited on the floor. Or maybe someone just died.* I reached into my bag to grab another peppermint candy.

On the bed in room 816, wrapped in sterile plastic packaging, was my complimentary, ass-hanging-out-of-the-back hospital gown. *Fuck. This day just keeps getting better and better.* Andrew ducked out of the room. I placed my nude pumps beside the chair and hung my blazer and pinstriped pants in the mini-closet. My arms threaded through the openings, and I tied the string around my torso. *Wow—this is symbolic. Time to surrender.*

Andrew returned to the room with an orderly pushing a cot. "What's this?" I asked.

"What do you mean? It's a cot," Andrew said, like I was an idiot.

"What do you mean, what do I mean? Why is it here?" I asked.

"I'm not going anywhere," he said with an attitude. "I'm staying right here, with you. Buckle up, baby. You wanted us to live together. Here you go."

"You don't have to," I replied, trying to hide my overwhelming wish to have him stand by my side—forever.

"Deb, I'm not going anywhere." How could someone be so lucky and so unlucky at the same time?

It was only 2:00 p.m., but it seemed like the day had been going on forever. I'd called my mom a few times but her phone was going straight to voicemail. I suddenly remembered that she was giving a presentation in midtown. I left her another message. "Mom, I went to Dr. PC today. My platelet count is really low. I'm at Uptown hospital. Room 816. Come as soon as you get this."

Dr. R. walked in with a nurse holding several IV bags, and announced proudly, "We looked at your bone marrow and it appears to be normal. I don't think anything more serious than ITP is at play here. Let's get you started on Treatment #1." *Yes. Thank you, God. Yes.* "This will take a few hours today, and then we'll give you the second round tomorrow. We should see results within a few days. Side effects are minimal—you might get the chills or feel a bit drowsy." The nurse took my arm and began to examine the same abused vein that seemed to be the center of everyone's attention. I told her about its history and she graciously moved on to my other arm.

My mother ran into the room a little after 6:00 p.m. She was huffing and puffing, her hair was tossed, and her usual picture-perfect ensemble was disheveled. I did my best to fill her in on the day's events. "They gave you a bone marrow biopsy?! Oh babe, I'm so sorry," she softly exhaled. She wanted to take it all away.

With the cloud of cancer lifted, the entire experience just felt different than the first time I entered the hospital world. Yes, of course I was scared—a spontaneous brain bleed was freakin' terrifying, but the doctors and nurses were smiling and walking in and out of my room with ease. No one had the holy-shit-how-do-I-tell-this-girl-she-could-die look. The enemy had a name, and the doctors had a plan of attack. I felt like I could handle anything they threw at me, as long as cancer wasn't in the title. I remembered the woman at the Information

Desk ten years ago—the look in her eyes would haunt
me forever. But no one was looking at me that way now.
This was an extreme turn of events, but manageable.
I can do this.

That first night in the hospital was a smooth one.
Like Dr. R said, there were no unfortunate side effects. I
was mildly anxious, slightly nauseated and my forehead
broke out with little red bumps. All tolerable. With
Andrew and my mother beside me, I watched television
and read through every gossip magazine sold in the
hospital gift shop. By 3:00 p.m., the IV bag was empty
and the treatment was complete. *Now we wait.* A blood
count was taken that evening. "Deb, you're at 6,000.
The medicine hasn't kicked in yet. It needs time to do
its job." The next morning we waited for the machine
to pop out my numbers. "It's still 6,000. We're going to
wait another day, but it's likely we'll have to move onto
the second regiment. It's a steroid protocol that is taken
orally. We slam you with a large initial dose and then
wean you off slowly for four days. But let's give your
body until tomorrow and see what happens." Dr. R
called it a night.

Day 3. Morning numbers came in at 5,000. *Steroid
time.* Dr. R started Treatment #2, which made me feel
bizarre and hungry. My fear of a spontaneous brain
bleed was now compounded by this new crazy. Andrew
went home to shower, get some work done, and pack
more clothes. Neither of us had expected to be in the
hospital this long. As I waited for my platelets to start

multiplying over the next several days, I conducted Ben & Jerry's taste tests in my hospital room (the nurses were nice enough to keep my pints of heaven in their freezer) and watched way too much reality television.

Day 6. No change. *Shit. What if they can't fix this? What if my brain explodes tonight?*

Day 7. 4,000.

Day 8. 6,000.

Day 9. 2,000. This was not good.

Day 10. 5,000. It was clear my body wasn't responding the way the doctors had hoped.

Dr. R walked in for morning rounds and informed us that he was going to administer ITP Treatment #3, a one-shot injection. "And what if it doesn't work?" I asked.

"Then we'll have to consult with the surgical team." Dr. R explained how my spleen could hold the answer to my platelet predicament. "But first, let's give you the injection, allow it to work over the course of the weekend, and see what happens." *Please, please, please work.*

Day 13. Monday morning arrived and I awoke to Andrew's head in his hands.

"What's wrong?"

"You're at 5,000. It didn't work."

"Fuck!" I yelled. I was losing confidence that my ITP was something that could be beaten. For two weeks I had stayed the course, but now I was absolutely exhausted and had nothing to show for it.

"The surgical team is going to talk to us about the splenectomy. They're thinking maybe tomorrow," Andrew informed me.

"I have plans tomorrow," I said sarcastically. He grinned. I grinned back.

Day 15. An escort arrived at 6:00 a.m. to bring me to the operating room. I unhappily disrobed from my yellow and pink floral pjs and donned the hospital gown.

"I guess I need to get on that thing?" I asked, semi-annoyed, referring to the gurney outside my door.

"Yes," came the reply, "It's hospital policy." *Of course it is.*

We rolled down the hallway, into the elevator, and descended four flights. Approaching the "Authorized Personnel Only" sign, the wheels stopped. The escort directed my mother and Andrew towards the waiting room. "She will meet you in recovery." They both leaned down to kiss me—it took all of my strength to not get up out of that godforsaken bed and run like hell.

"Hopefully, ITP will meet its match today. I love you." The automatic doors opened and I was, once again, alone. *I hate this. I really hate this. This better work.*

They slid me from the gurney onto the operating table in one swift maneuver. While his team zipped around the room, the surgeon greeted me and explained exactly what he was going to do and where the incisions would be. I appreciated his clear and informative way of speaking. Someone asked me to count down from ten, and the next thing I saw were Andrew and my mom smiling over me in the recovery room. She squeezed my hand. "It went really well. You're doing great. Just rest." Maybe five minutes later, or thirty minutes later, or sixty minutes later, I realized I needed to pee. I tried to speak but it was too difficult. The nurse saw that I was struggling to communicate.

"Don't try to speak. Just rest," she repeated.

I managed to eek out, "But I need to pee."

"Oh, okay. Let me get you a bedpan."

Oh man. She slid the plastic receptacle under my body as I tried my best to elevate my lower half. *Okay, pee Deb.* I heard loud beeps, someone crying, and twenty different people talking at once. I couldn't concentrate.

"Did you go?" asked the nurse.

"Not yet," I responded. *Relax, just pee.*

"Are you done yet?"

"No!" I snapped.

"Well, we're going to be bringing you up to your room in a few minutes so you can go up there if you would like." *Lady, what I'd like is some privacy.* By the time I was wheeled to my room, my bladder was about to explode. I kicked everyone out immediately so I could pee in peace.

My spleen had been removed without complication. An hour after surgery, my blood count came in at 84,000. At 6:00 p.m., the nurse drew my blood. At 7:00 p.m., Dr. R walked in. "Deb, I'm so sorry, but it's back to 25,000. The last read probably included the IV platelets you received in surgery. The splenectomy was unsuccessful." I began to cry. Andrew put his head in the crux of my neck and my mother approached Dr. R.

"What does that mean?" she asked, turning from soft and feminine into a warrior queen.

"It means we need to rethink the past two weeks and try to determine why your body is failing the treatments."

Excuse me? Buddy, the only thing I have ever failed in my life was a ridiculous Business Law class during my junior year of college and that's because my professor was a douche. Are you seriously telling me that it's my body's fault that your treatments aren't working?!

Dr. R sat down beside me. "I'm concerned about our lack of progress. We need to confirm that there is nothing more *serious* at play here." *Ugh, that word again.* "I'd like to perform another bone marrow biopsy." *Double ugh.* It wasn't what he said that freaked me out— it was how he said it. *I'm scared. Why can't they figure this out? Am I going to die?*

"Can I at least get some drugs for the pain, Dr. R?"

"I think we can arrange for some Ativan." *Thank God for small favors.*

The needle went in—twist, pop, and out came another chunk of my bone marrow. I was shaking from the inside out. I think the nurse took pity on me. She gave me something to help me relax and I passed out. Andrew and I didn't make a sound that night. We just held our breath and hoped.

Day 22. Dr. R walked into my room shortly after daybreak. He hadn't even begun to speak. I knew what cancer looked like in someone else's eyes. I took a deep breath and listened. "Deb, the biopsy came back and you do not have ITP. We found a genetic abnormality in some of your bone marrow. You have something called Myelodysplastic Syndrome (MDS). We consider it a pre-cancer. It was most likely caused by the chemotherapy you received when you were a teenager. It's only treatment, unfortunately, is a bone marrow transplant." Tears poured down my face. I wanted to pull my knees to my chest but could barely move since I was still recovering from surgery. I didn't care about the pain in that moment. I wanted to literally curl up in a ball and hide. *One cancer's treatment is another cancer's cause. What kind of evil is this?* Dr. R spoke in a steady, matter-of-fact tone and explained what a bone marrow transplant actually entailed. I struggled not to pass out. Sobbing, I pleaded with him.

"Dr. R, I don't want to die. Please. I want to marry this man and have babies with him. I'll do whatever you tell me to do. I'll do it all—chemo, transplant, whatever—just please don't let me die." The unshakable Dr. R filled up with tears. His armor melted and he held my hand. My head collapsed into my palms. *Why? Why is this happening?* Why save my life once, allowing me to fall in love, dream about a future filled with magnificent moments like our wedding, our first home, our parents becoming grandparents, family ski trips, Thanksgiving dinners spent watching football and eating pie, only to be told, "Ha! Joke's on you sucker!" *No! No! No!*

Focus, Deb. Focus. Try to listen. I wasn't being asked to sit here and die. I was being asked to go through hell and then maybe live. I tried to take a deep breath. It felt like every single organ in my body, besides my spleen, that is, was trembling with fear.

Chapter 12

The Resurgence of the Trapper Keeper

I DID MY BEST to compose myself and grabbed the pen I'd been using in that morning's game of Hangman. I wrote on the back of a support group flyer. "What is this disease called?" I asked.

"It's called Myelodysplastic Syndrome."

"And that is? In words I can understand."

"The cells in your bone marrow are mutating, and as they multiply and take over your marrow, you will stop producing the red and white blood cells your body needs to survive. A bone marrow transplant is the only treatment."

"Walk me through the transplant. How is it performed? How long does it take?" I asked robotically.

"We need to remove and replace your bone marrow, which is the basis for your immune system. You'll be moved into a transplant room while we kill off your marrow, and then replace it with someone else's. A match."

As I continued to spit out questions, Dr. R could hardly keep up. What did it mean to have a bone marrow match? How did you find a match? Did it hurt? Would I be in isolation? For how long? Could I listen to music or watch TV? Could my family visit me? But under the surface, the vital yet unspoken question haunted me like no other: Would I survive?

"Once the marrow is completely destroyed," Dr. R. continued, "your body is left without an immune system and is obviously subject to all kinds of danger. Because of this susceptibility, you must remain in total isolation." *Total isolation?* I felt alone to begin with. Now he was telling me that I couldn't even have someone hold my hand. Dr. R explained that once we found a match, I'd be given his or her bone marrow cells intravenously, and my immune system would rebuild. I was so petrified I couldn't even think.

"Do you have any siblings?" Dr. R. asked.

"Yes, I have a brother," I replied.

"We'll start by testing him. There's a twenty-five percent chance that he's a match. If he's not, we move on to the national registry." *What if no one's a match?*

I furiously wrote down every word as Dr. R explained the bone marrow matching process. "Mom, I need a new pen," I said. There was silence. "I need a pen—I'm out of ink!" I barked. Dr. R quickly gave me the one attached to his lapel and we continued. In two hours, my life had turned upside down once again. It's funny how you think you're having a shitty day and then something else happens, and it's like someone saying, "Nope, that wasn't really shitty. *This* is really shitty."

Dr. R sent my mother, Andrew, and me up to the transplant floor for a preview of what was to come. Thankfully, our escort didn't bring us past any active patients; more appropriately, she showed us an empty room. She proudly pointed to the bed, bathroom, bookshelves, and an iPod dock, which were all surrounded by a plastic bubble. Thick gloves were encased in the hallway wall reaching inside the room. It looked like something out of a sci-fi movie.

"What do you think?" asked the guide.

"What do I think?" I responded, enunciating each syllable. "This is totally fucked up! That is what I think. I don't mean to be rude but I've been here for twenty-two days, had at least fifty blood tests, and received tons of medication that didn't work because the doctors were treating the wrong disease. I had an organ surgically removed for no good reason. And now…now it turns out that I actually have something so much worse. And I might die. I think I want to lie on the ground, right here, and scream. I think I want to jump out the fucking window and end it all. That's what I think!" I turned around and stomped towards the elevators. "I'm going back to my room," I yelled to whoever was listening.

I met my mom and Andrew back in Room 816 after I cooled off. A tall man I'd never seen before entered with a sheepish grin.

"Hello?" I asked.

"Deborah. I'm Dr. Crazy. I'm a psychiatrist." *Oh shit.* When the words poured out of my mouth an hour earlier, I wasn't considering the consequences. I was a goddamn social worker—I knew better than to yell, for the whole hospital to hear, that I wanted to "end it all."

"I know why you're here," I said. "I'm sorry for making a scene. I wasn't actually going to jump out of the ninth floor window. Have you seen my chart? It's been a messed up few weeks." I attempted to appear as sane as possible. He must have determined that I wasn't going to harm myself or others because he eventually left.

That evening we set up an appointment to meet the transplant team at Downtown Hospital. Maybe it was the weeks of failed treatments for the wrong disease. Maybe it was the lack of apologies for the misdiagnosis. Maybe it was the chick on the transplant floor that spoke like she was doing me a favor. Or maybe I was just trying to run. Either way, we were out of there.

Day 23. I put on something other than pajamas for the first time in almost a month. I had dreamt of the day I'd be discharged, but I never imagined it would be on these terms. The cab ride from Uptown Hospital to Downtown Hospital was not part of my dream. We walked to the new facility with purpose, went straight up to the hematology/oncology floor, and reported to the front desk. *Here we go again. Cancer.*

At Downtown Hospital, my fate was in Dr. P's hands. She was 5'10" with curly brown hair and heavy eye make-up. She met us in an exam room and got right down to business.

"Hello, Deborah. I have your latest counts from Uptown Hospital and understand that you've been inpatient for a month for ITP," she confirmed. "And now a bone marrow biopsy indicates that you don't have ITP, but MDS."

"Yes," I responded.

"And your counts have never gone above 8,000 in that time frame?" she asked.

"Correct," I said.

Dr. P fired off questions about my Hodgkin's history and the past month's ordeal. "With a platelet count less than 10,000, you could have a spontaneous bleed at any time and if that bleed is in your brain we have big trouble." *Where had I heard that before?*

"When you were uptown, they never gave you a transfusion?" she asked.

"Only during surgery," I responded. "They said my body would just destroy fresh cells so they didn't think it was worth it."

"I looked at your bone marrow slide from Uptown Hospital and it does reflect an abnormality indicating MDS. However, we'd like to conduct our own test, in our own lab, to confirm the results before we proceed."

I knew what that meant. "Another biopsy. Now?" I asked.

"Yes, right now." I made my mother leave the room. I unbuckled my jeans and positioned myself on my stomach. Andrew held my hand and I felt the cold alcohol swipe clockwise.

"This is going to pinch," she said. *Pinch? Brace yourself.* The corkscrew went in—hard. Then it was over.

Dr. P was all action. "Okay, here's the plan. We need to test your brother to see if he's a match. We need to wait for this biopsy to confirm the MDS diagnosis, which will take a few days. I'm not comfortable with your platelet count. I'd like to give you a platelet transfusion and then you can go home."

"I can go home?" I asked, surprised.

"Yes, there's no reason you need to be inpatient at this point. You need to come back tomorrow though." *I'll take it!*

I looked at my nails and said under my breath, "I need a manicure so badly."

Dr. P heard me. "Sorry, Deb," she said, "your nails need to remain polish-free because certain symptoms present through the nail bed." Some things are too good to be true. I *almost* laughed at my predicament.

In a few hours, I would get to go to the bathroom without an IV pole. I would get to shave my legs in my *own* shower. Oh wait, I wasn't allowed to shave because of the sharp blade—shit. Well, at least I could take a bath in private. I longed for my own pillow. In order for the doctors to consent to my release, I had to promise to limit my activity to walking around the block once a day and to make absolutely no use of kitchen knives. I didn't care. I was going home!

I had quite the to-do list and Robert was my first phone call. My brother had been to the hospital several times to check up on me. He brought me sweet treats from my favorite bakeries and flirted with every nurse on the floor. Now I had to call him and ask for this enormous favor, but first I had to tell him why. I hated making this phone call. I didn't have time to console or assure him. *I hate this.* I updated Robert on where things stood and what I needed from him. Thankfully, he was his true, no-bullshit self.

"I'm so sorry," he said.

"I know, I know. It hasn't sunk in yet. Can you come today?" I asked.

"I'll be there in thirty minutes."

My brother walked into the exam room where I was sitting with my mom and Andrew.

"Shit, Deb," he said. "This is really fucked up."

"Yeah, I know," I said with a nod.

"Hi, are you the brother?" a nurse asked.

"That's me," Robert responded with a gleaming smile. It didn't hurt that the nurse happened to be 5'9", curvy, and blonde. Robert left with her.

"He's unbelievable," I chuckled. While my brother was in one room getting his blood drawn, my platelets arrived and I was prepped for the transfusion. I signed the consent form and the platelets streamed in through my IV. It only took a few hours from start to finish. As we were packing up to leave, Dr. P informed us that my platelets were up 26,000 from the transfusion. I almost leapt out of my seat with excitement.

"What does that mean?" I asked.

"It means you're at a lower risk for a spontaneous bleed and we hope your body can retain the new platelets. We'll see you tomorrow."

The last few weeks were a godforsaken mess. It was the first night in my own bed. After a long, hot shower, I turned my purse upside down and emptied its contents onto my bedroom floor. Papers flew out one after the other. *Here's the packet explaining the transplant. It's a lot of information. How will this be different than chemo? Will I lose my hair during a transplant? Am I allowed to eat cupcakes? Where are all those pieces of paper with notes scribbled on them? Where is that sheet the doctor gave me? Oh, here's the living will. Fabulous. Deb, slow down.* It was time to regroup, time to organize and gain some control over the chaos in my mind. A bone marrow transplant was a *big* deal.

The next morning I woke up with Andrew beside me. We grabbed freshly brewed lattes at Starbucks and I told Andrew we needed to make a quick stop.

"We need to see Dr. P in twenty minutes, Deb," he said.

"I know. We won't be late. Just c'mon." I took his hand and dragged him through the doors of CVS. I'm sure he thought I needed an economy size bottle of antacids. I grabbed a cart and headed straight to the scotch tape aisle.

When I was a little girl, the end of summer was always a time filled with anxiety. A new school year was about to begin, bringing homework, tests, spelling bees, projects, and angst. I was the kind of student who studied for hours, memorizing vocabulary words and state capitals, and at the end of the day frustratingly only received a B. In my house, A's meant you were bright and studied hard, which would pave the way to acceptance into a good college, which then translated into becoming a successful adult and a happy human being. Memorizing information (which was the basic method of first through eighth grade) wasn't my strong suit. My mind wandered, I would have preferred to be outside creating my own worlds of drama and discovery. But every August, I'd try my best to prepare for the upcoming year. As in most households across America, my mother would take me to Rite Aid and I would stock up on pencils, pens, highlighters, folders, notebooks, paper clips, stickers, book covers, and, of course, the pièce de résistance—the Trapper Keeper. It was the master of organizational tools, and it made me feel like I had it all together and could tackle the challenges ahead. Barbie folders, colored highlighters, and pretty labels all served as a medium for me to positively connect to my academics. This became an annual rite of passage. So why not give it a try again? And so began the resurgence of the Trapper Keeper.

We returned to Downtown hospital with CVS bags filled with My Little Pony folders, tons of paper (white and construction), a pack of colored highlighters, and a new package of blue Bic pens. I also treated myself to one of those funky markers with the fluffy tops that I always wanted when I was eight. I'm twenty-eight—I could get the damn pen if I wanted it! And of course, the outer layer which holds all within—the Trapper Keeper.

We proceeded straight to the sixth floor. Unlike yesterday, I was now an official patient sitting in a waiting room surrounded by the fifty other people who needed blood work. When my name was finally called, I approached a man, 6'3" and 250 lbs., with tattoos peeking out of his scrubs.

"Hi, I'm Sal," he said. "Take a seat."

I nodded. Pointing to my left arm, I said, "Just don't use this one. I know it looks delicious. It's not."

"Thanks for the info. Your first day?" he asked.

"My second. Well, at least at this hospital."

"Yeah, a lot of people here have that kind of story." As Sal extracted the needle and gave me a neon pink band aid, he said, "Nice meeting you."

"Likewise."

I joined Andrew back in the waiting room and my mother arrived minutes thereafter. "Good morning," Dr. P greeted us. "Why don't you follow me." It's never a good sign when the doctor doesn't want to discuss something in front of others. "Unfortunately, your platelet count is back down to 4,000. So, we will plan on giving you another transfusion tomorrow if it doesn't increase throughout the day."

"Okay," I said. "So when am I going into isolation? When is the transplant going to begin?"

"We need to wait until your bone marrow biopsy results come back. We will also have your brother's results in a few days, but remember, there is only a one-in-four chance that he's a match. If we need to, we will then look at the national registry. We're just going to have to take this day-by-day. Your job is to go home and rest."

"I'll try," I said.

The three of us took a cab to my apartment. We unpacked all my new supplies and started to consolidate the pile of paperwork still sprawled across my floor. I opened up the lime-green Trapper Keeper and placed my "Welcome to Cancerville" brochure in the cover folder along with "Bone Marrow Transplant 101." Then I began to create a calendar for the first section. You'd think that getting stuck with a needle the size of the Washington Monument would leave a date engrained in your memory, but it's incredible how quickly you do, in fact, forget. I needed to know exactly when and where all my biopsies took place, as well as keep track of all appointments, procedures, surgeries, rounds of medication, inpatient days at the hospital, outpatient days, transfusions, and consultations with various specialists. Having everything recorded in one place would help me when Dr. P (or anyone else, for that matter) had a specific question. I could whip out my calendar and bam—there you go.

The second section was filled with pages and pages of loose-leaf paper. Questions, answers, concerns, dates of surgery, doodles—I wrote it all down. I marked the top of every page with a date. I wrote down every question I could possibly think of. Whether at 4:00 a.m.

or 2:00 p.m., I pulled out the notebook section and started to write. I even slept with the Trapper Keeper under my pillow because during the night, when the world was quiet, my mind would wander. It's crazy how you can be sitting in a consultation room with a surgeon, and two hours later not remember a single thing he said. I wrote:

What is MDS?

How many kinds of this disease are there?

What are the treatment options?

What are the side effects of medication?

What tests need to be administered for diagnosis?

Who runs the tests? The hospital itself? A lab in Nebraska? Where?

How long does the transplant take?

The BIG question—what are my odds of survival?

My life was becoming more overwhelming by the minute. Fortunately, the color-coded charts, lists of questions followed by the answers from the medical team, and my folders of resources, allowed me to focus and prepare for the next step.

As I read about bone marrow transplants, I almost laughed at the amount of medication I'd be ingesting on a daily basis. And the sequencing of the meds was critical. One needed to be tapered down every day for five days. The softener needed to be taken twice a day but not on Sundays. The dosage, quantity, timing, and mixing of each of these drugs was a juggling act. There were so many different sequences that I needed a way to keep my pill popping on a safe track. So the third section was going to be my medication log.

I stepped back and looked to see what had yet to be filed. My Health Care Proxy and Last Will and Testament were still sitting on the floor. I felt like they were speaking to me: "Where do we belong?" *Nowhere!* I shoved them into the back folder and closed my Trapper Keeper.

Chapter 13

Day 62

DAY 30. IT WAS my fifth day at Downtown hospital. I'd received two platelet transfusions and was awaiting my third visit with Sal. He bellowed from across the waiting room, "Deb, I'm going to be a few minutes." I decided to call Vicki, tell her the news, and ask her to start the phone chain because I didn't have it in me to make the calls myself. No one knew about the MDS diagnosis yet or that I'd transferred hospitals. After uttering a few key sentences, she asked, "What can I do?"

"You can visit me at my new home in the bubble. Apparently my room has an iPod dock. You can watch me dance through the glass doors," I said trying to lighten the mood. "I'm ready for you!" Sal called. "Gotta go, Vick. Love you."

"Good morning. You're an early riser," he said as he stuck the needle in and quickly filled up four vials. *He's a pro.* I met Andrew and my mom in the waiting room, and Dr. P greeted us shortly thereafter.

"You are a tricky one," she said.

"I'm a what?" I asked.

"Come with me," she said, already walking towards her office. *Oh Shit! Her office! That's even worse than an exam room.* Her face was stern and I was sure she was going to tell me it was time for the isolation chamber. I'd been working on convincing myself that I was going on vacation and that packing my bags wasn't such a big deal— just a quick trip to "Casa De Bone Marrow" and I'd get to go back to my real life. Dr. P opened her mouth—"The results of your biopsy came back...they are negative," she said. For a second I couldn't remember which one was the bad one—negative or positive. Negative sounds like it would be bad but it's actually good!

"Negative? Negative for what?" I asked just to clear things up.

"Negative for MDS," she responded. "I'm not sure what's going on. What I do know is that your platelet count is back down to a critical level. It's 3,000 today. I know you don't want to hear this but we need to do another biopsy." I couldn't breathe. I couldn't stand. I couldn't speak. I put my head between my legs and didn't know if I should laugh or cry. "So I might not have MDS?" I asked apprehensively.

"I think you do have MDS. I think something went wrong with this test. We need to do another one." My heart plummeted. I pulled my pants down. *Here we go.* Needle, extraction, band aid. "Oh, and your brother is a match," she said. *What?!* My feelings were bouncing from high anticipation, to depression, to excitement, back to a black hole and now…gratitude. The three of us collectively hugged.

Dr. P was sending my marrow slides to some of her colleagues in California and D.C. so it was going to take a few extra days to get the results. We waited. Trying to withstand the tornado that had reached out and grabbed me, my mind continuously wandered. I kept thinking back to the first bone marrow biopsy. As a patient, I often felt like I couldn't question medical authority or oppose their direction. Would they get mad? Would that affect their treatment of me, even if it was subconscious? I was scared to bring up the original biopsy because historically, my questions were uninvited. Nonetheless, my gut said that you don't need to be a rocket scientist to understand that when the blue team scores a point and then the red team scores a point, it's called a tie. Any second grader could tell you that! And look—it was right there in my Trapper Keeper. At one point I had asked the Uptown Hospital about a third test, but I was told it wasn't necessary. The medical team felt the second test was sufficient and there was no reason to doubt its viability. I was given looks; I was doubted and undermined. I was still scared out of my mind, but at the same time I felt like I'd finally woken up. I considered my role as a patient, the doctor's responsibilities, and how we co-exist in this complicated construct. I wasn't a child anymore. I had traveled through the healthcare system and I was ready to take the beast by the horns.

That night, I recorded my enlightened thoughts in my Trapper Keeper. I was stronger and clearer. I woke up armed for battle once again. I got dressed and put on my black leather boots with the silver buckle. I didn't care if they were impractical. I hadn't worn shoes in months and had no idea if I was going to be admitted to the hospital before the sun went down. So I took the opportunity to wear the boots that made me feel kick-ass, especially since I wasn't permitted to apply the Slay The Dragon Red that was calling my name. I made my way to the hospital for my daily platelet count.

"Morning, Sal."

"I thought you were heading over to Casa De Bone Marrow today," he said, clearly impressed with himself for remembering my reference.

"I thought so, too. They still can't confirm my diagnosis, so I'm in limbo. But my platelets are all messed up, so here I am. Again."

Andrew, my voice of reason, was on a work call and my mom and I waited for the doctor. A nurse came over a few minutes later and told us Dr. P was in a consultation but was recommending a platelet transfusion since my numbers were 6,000.

"Mom, I don't think I want to do it."

"What do you mean?" she asked.

"I mean my body, whatever the condition, is taking my platelets and destroying them as fast as possible. Each time I've had a transfusion my numbers rose for twelve hours and then plummeted even lower. It's like there's a platelet monster inside me and once he sees blood, he goes crazy and eats even more of my supply. Does that make any sense?"

My mom desperately tried to understand what I was talking about. The nurse looked at me like I should be sent to the psych ward instead of the transplant floor. "I'm just saying, what's the use of the transfusion if it's only good for a few hours? I have to sign this waiver every time. I'm trying to weigh the factors here."

"Do you want me to tell the doctor you're refusing the transfusion?" the nursed asked.

"No, I'm not refusing the transfusion. I just want to discuss the thought process behind it."

"I'll be right back," replied the nurse as she walked away.

"Deborah, I get it. What's the medical opinion?" she asked.

"That's what I'm trying to find out, but I guess their opinion is twelve hours of healthy platelets is better than nothing."

The nurse returned. "Okay, Dr. P is fine with whatever you want to do and you can come back on Monday."

"But that's not what I was asking," I said in annoyance. *Deep breath.*

"What do you want to do?" Mom asked.

"I want to go home, but I hope I'm making the right decision."

"Okay, then let's go. We'll be back after the weekend."

Day 36. "The slides haven't come back yet, but we

need a plan," explained Dr. P. "If the results are positive, we will admit you immediately and begin the transplant process. If they are negative, well…we still need to deal with your platelet count. I've been researching platelet conditions and have identified a drug. It's actually a cancer drug called Rituximab. Its main mission is to destroy your B cells. So, for conditions like ITP which need B cells to survive, the drug could potentially eradicate the disease. Rituximab is administered intravenously once a week for four weeks. I don't know if this is going to work since I still believe you have MDS, but I think we need to take action and address your critically low platelet count." *I think I'm spinning.* "Deb, I'm navigating unchartered territory here." *I'm definitely spinning.* "Let's see what happens with the biopsy and we'll go from there," she said. I nodded.

Waiting for the results was painful. We didn't know what to do with ourselves. I'd never felt so many emotions at one time. I was so happy to be sleeping in my bed. I'm sure the miraculous news that I might not have this ass-biting disease was also generating a ray of hope and optimism within me, but Dr. P's opinions on the MDS/ITP discussion were plaguing me. *Please, please, please.*

Day 40. The phone woke us up at 8:00 a.m. "What time is it?" Andrew asked as I rolled over to grab the cordless.

"Hello Deborah, It's Dr. P."

"Oh, hi. How are you?" I asked instinctively.

"Your slides came back. No one could find any signs of MDS in your sample. Your cells don't look perfectly normal but they do not show MDS. Deborah, are you there?" she asked.

"I'm here. I'm here" I said, breathing heavily as Andrew wiped the tears from my face. "So, the only thing we know for sure is that your platelet count needs help. I would like to start you on Rituximab—tomorrow. Is that okay with you?" she asked.

"Yes, of course." I replied.

A few weeks before my 29th birthday, I woke up at 7:00 a.m., changed into sweatpants and a sweatshirt, and headed to the hospital. By 9:00 a.m., I was sitting in an outpatient treatment room, where a technician inserted my IV. The pre-drugs included a hefty dose of Benadryl.

"Am I going to fall asleep?" I asked.

"Maybe, it depends," she said.

"Depends on…" Going, going, going, gone. I was out. I woke up as they exchanged bags of clear liquid for different bags of clear liquid. I was out again. Around 4:00 p.m., a nurse disconnected all the tubes from my body and we went home. I arrived forty-eight hours later for a CBC—6,000. A few days later—6,000. *Is the Rituximab unsuccessful because I do, in fact, have MDS? Or do I have ITP and I'm just going to die of a brain bleed because no medication can cure me? Breathe, Deb.*

Day 48. It was time for my second treatment. *Please work this time. Please.* They loaded me up, I slept, and we went home. A few days later, I entered Sal's saloon and, like a bartender asking me about my day, we made small talk (that wasn't so small) while I held out my arm and he filled up his vials. Dr. P thought that if we didn't see results after the second dose, it probably wasn't going to work. "Make it a good one, Sal. Get that blood. And tell it not to disappoint." *This is it. Last shot. C'mon.*

I sat with my mother, brother, and Andrew in the waiting room. Dr. P walked in with a blank face. *Don't get excited.*

"It's 23,000," she stated, smiling. *Yes!* It was working. My platelet count had bounced between 1,000 and 8,000 over the past three months, averaging approximately 4,000. I hadn't been in the twenty thousands since all of this had started. We celebrated with turkey sandwiches, chips and water at the corner deli. It was the most delicious meal.

"I love you," Andrew said as we walked down Lexington Avenue.

"I love you, too," I said.

Day 55. I almost skipped into the infusion room. I wanted the drug like I wanted a huge piece of seven-layer cake. *Give it to me!* The next CBC read 68,000. "Yes! Yes! Yes!" I screamed in the hallway and then ran over to Sal to give him a hug.

Dr. P explained, "The fact that the Rituximab is working proves that you do have ITP. Rituximab would not cure MDS. However, we cannot ignore that one positive slide. Let's give it a few weeks, finish the treatments, see where your platelets are and then do another biopsy."

"No problem," I agreed with a smile.

Day 62. By the fourth and last treatment, my counts were up to 90,000. *This is a good day!* I felt like I had won the lottery. And it was time for my fifth biopsy. It was negative.

They ran yet another test a month later. Negative again. My team concluded, with certainty, that the second biopsy, the only positive result, was in fact incorrect. The five additional tests that came back negative were paramount. I didn't have cancer, or pre-cancer. The scariest part of the whole experience—the part that will always send a chill up my spine—was that the person who insisted on the third biopsy was me. What would have happened if I'd entered the isolation room without getting a second opinion? *Note to self: take charge of your own life—no exceptions.*

Monthly follow-up appointments were the only remaining evidence of this whole disastrous saga. I knew better than to immediately jump back into my life. And just in case my brain forgot, my body reminded me. I had a handful of panic attacks and some generalized anxiety. How would I re-enter the world again? I took almost a year off to figure out that question. I saw a therapist and talked everything out. I explored every emotion and asked questions about things I hadn't had time to acknowledge. What the hell is ITP? Why didn't the drugs work? What does the spleen do? Why didn't anyone trust the first bone marrow test? Why didn't anyone use the word mistake? Who is responsible for this atrocity? How do I just move on?

I took the time I needed to reintegrate back into society. I learned to cook something other than a pot full of spaghetti with canned tomato sauce. I crocheted a baby blanket for Kim's unborn child and I took out my nail kit, which had sadly collected a thick layer of dust. I finally mastered the French manicure. And then, once I was ready—really ready, I went back to work.

Chapter 14

To Have and To Hold

ONCE THE ITP MESS settled down, Andrew and I moved in together. I never slept more soundly than when we shared a bed. As fate would have it, some higher power heard my plea for a future with the man I loved.

It was Thanksgiving, 2007. Andrew and I were heading out to my family's apartment in New Jersey. Bundled in layers of scarves and down jackets, we were almost blown over by the wind on our way to the car.

"Did you know Thanksgiving is my favorite holiday?" I asked Andrew.

"Really? Well, that makes sense," he replied.

"Why?" I asked.

"Because it's the happiest holiday there is. It's about family, food, and football. It has you written all over it."

"I wonder if my mom will let me sneak a piece of pumpkin pie before dinner." I asked.

"Um, no. Have you met your mother?" Andrew said with certainty.

"A girl can dream." We laughed.

We walked into the apartment and kissed everyone. My mom was in the kitchen checking on the turkey, my uncle was pouring himself a glass of wine, and my brother was getting out of the shower. "Why are you getting out of the shower? You don't live here. You know what—never mind," I chuckled. Thanksgiving is all about being with your family and enjoying the crazy. While my cousin was smashing the sweet potatoes, Andrew slyly glanced my way.

"Why are you looking at me like that?" I asked.

"Because I have a surprise," he said.

"Oh?" I asked.

"Well, I hope you're not mad, but we're not staying for dinner."

"We're not?" I asked.

"No, a car is picking us up in an hour."

"Where are we going?"

"I'm not telling you!"

"Seriously?"

"Seriously."

Staring at my family I asked, "Do you guys know?!"

"Yep," they all said in unison.

I stared out the window as the driver crossed back over the George Washington Bridge and down the FDR. "Are we going to a restaurant? A hotel? An S&M bar?"

"I'm not telling you," he balked. Twenty minutes later, the car pulled into the driveway of our apartment building.

"What's going on? Tell me you didn't drag me away from turkey, stuffing, and pumpkin pie to come to our apartment?" I was pissy.

"Give me a little credit," Andrew said. "We're here to pack."

"Pack? For where? Okay, at least tell me what climate."

"For this climate," he said. After fifteen minutes, I'd thrown my favorite sweaters, jeans and boots into a suitcase and headed back to the car.

"Are we going to the airport?!" I asked.

"Nope." The car continued to make its way through Queens.

"But it looks like we're going to the airport."

"Nope." Thirty minutes passed and we pulled into JFK terminal.

"We *are* going to the airport."

"Yep."

"You're relentless!" I yelled.

We rolled our bags through security and my heart was pounding. Where was he taking me? What was he up to? We got all the way to the gate without the proverbial beans being spilled, but finally, there was nowhere to hide. It was written right there on the gate sign—"Welcome all passengers to Flight 896 from JFK to Paris." Paris!

Almost six years after our momentous chance meeting in Turks and Caicos, Andrew bent down on one knee and proposed. The sun was setting behind the Louvre and the world went silent. The footsteps of pedestrians, motorcycle engines, and clock tower bells evaporated in an instant. All I could hear was the beating of my own heart and my soul screaming, "Yes, yes, yes!"

Andrew would have flown back to New York and taken a cab straight to City Hall, but I wanted the ceremony, the flowers, and a kick-ass party. I wanted to celebrate our incredible life together. The most important item on my to-do list was, of course, the dress. I walked into Saks Fifth Avenue with my mom and soon-to-be mother-in-law, Ina, in the hopes of finding some direction in a vast sea of options. We were greeted by a lovely woman named Bridgette who gave me a golden kernel of bridal insight. "You are going to try on lots of gowns today. All of them will be beautiful, but you need to decide whom you want to feel like on your wedding day. Some girls come in here and want to feel like a princess. Some want to feel like a beach goddess. Who are you? Be open. Let me help you." I stood there for a moment and let her words sink in. I quietly recited *gown...gown...gown...*I had been calling it a wedding dress, but it's not—it's a wedding gown. I'd been asked to change into a hospital gown hundreds of times. It symbolized vulnerability and was associated with fear, pain and mortality. I flashed back to when my friends were shopping for prom dresses and I was held up in a hospital bed with a terrifying infection. I remembered seeing the pictures of flowing taffeta and glistening silk and couldn't help but compare it to my own attire. The term backless dress meant something very different to me. *Deb, you're here now, and nothing is taking away this moment.*

As Bridgette brought in dress after dress, Ina, my mom, and I oohed and ahhed. One sparkled like a chandelier. Another draped like it belonged to Venus herself. I listened to Bridgette and focused on what the dress made me feel like. *Who am I in this one?* I stood in front of the mirror wearing one of my favorites. It was a strapless, lace-embroidered mermaid silhouette with boning throughout. It was beautiful. I played with my hair in the mirror, pulling my long, blonde highlighted tresses back into a bun. Then Bridgette asked if I wanted to try on the dress that was hanging in front of the showroom. I wouldn't have chosen it myself because it seemed kind of plain on the hanger and I wanted something fabulous. She handed me the white satin-silk sheath with a ten-foot train. Without a body inside, it could have folded up like a T-shirt. I placed my arms through the thin jeweled straps and Bridgette secured the delicate bindings. Its simplicity was stunning, its elegance unparalleled. *This is it!* The dress hugged my body and revealed my form. One hundred and ten pounds of me was on display—scars and all. There was no hiding, no shame. It reflected the balls-to-the-walls confidence that I had fought so hard to achieve. My mom and Ina may have liked other dresses, but they could both see how this gown made me feel. I looked strong and healthy, and felt sexy as hell. And that was exactly the bride that I wanted to be.

The day before the wedding, my mom, Ina, and my future sister-in-laws gathered at the Red Door Salon for mani-pedi sessions. We each piled into our comfy massage chairs and picked our colors. To honor elegance and tradition, I chose the classic French manicure and pedicure, which encapsulated the look, the dress, and the upcoming evening. My mind was clear and calm as we sipped champagne and enjoyed being pampered.

It was a beautiful snowy night in January. The fireplace roared and the white orchids were perfectly placed on every table. A good friend accepted our plea and became a licensed marriage officiant so that he could legally marry us in the State of New York. Our parents stood beside us, and our friends and family watched as we exchanged our vows. Andrew's openness, intelligence, warmth, and kindness made me a better person, and I just hoped I did the same for him. I saw myself in Andrew's eyes and had never felt more grounded. It was the truest moment I'd ever had. We were sitting in the pocket of a deep, enduring love…our very own forever.

Chapter 15

What do you mean it's positive?

I HAD BEEN SEEING Dr. H, a gynecology and fertility specialist, since I was sixteen years old. Because of the chemotherapy and radiation to my pelvic region, I was introduced to her almost immediately following the end of my treatment in 1994. Each year I took my annual trip over the George Washington Bridge to my hometown in New Jersey to see Dr. H. After hugs and greetings, she would say, "So, is there anyone special? Remember, these eggs aren't going to be there forever." Her comments were annoying as hell, but I knew she was just trying to protect me. I was all too clear on how my treatment could affect my reproductive health down the line. Dr. H made sure I understood that my obstetrical future was uncertain. Then she would run my blood and check my follicle stimulating hormone (FSH) number. I would likely experience early menopause, but early was never defined. It could be twenty-five, thirty-five, or forty-five—no one knew. Only time would tell. Everyone encouraged me to think about having children sooner rather than later.

At eighteen, twenty-one, and twenty-five years old, my FSH numbers remained stable. I was fertile. The future looked good.

I am a Gemini, which predisposes me to classical yin-yang behavior—opposing forces. Although that is the extent of my astrological knowledge, the characterization hits the nail on the head. Two lives, two characters trying to merge into one. In my twenties, I constantly wavered between two dreams. The first: to be normal. Work hard, play hard. The other was much more intense and complex. Girl number one wasn't ready to have children and even if Dr. H came in one day and told me that it was now or never, I still wouldn't have been ready. I didn't even have a boyfriend. A sperm donor at twenty-two? No thank you. However, if you spoke to the girl in the gown; the young woman who knew she wanted to be a mother since age six, the time pressure continued to plague me. Every month, when I saw those first few drops of blood marking the beginning of my period, I exhaled.

Six months after our wedding, I was lying in bed next to Andrew. "Honey, I'm ready," I calmly stated.

"Ready for what?" he asked.

"I'm ready to be woken up at 2:00 a.m., 4:00 a.m., and 6:00 a.m. I'm ready for diapers, first words, first days of school." He knew my decision was grounded in excitement, not fear or desperation.

He looked at me, smiled and replied, "Okay, let's check it out." So, the next week my blood was drawn.

Although my levels had been on the higher end of the spectrum for a few years, they were still within the fertile range. I had awaited these results every year for over a decade, but this was the first time they actually mattered. The call came and my numbers were through the roof. They weren't just high, but off the charts. And high meant bad. I started to cry. I refused to believe this was over. That this was it. *Not now. Please, not now.*

Within days, I booked appointments with the best fertility specialists in New York. I would have boarded a plane to Antarctica if I had to, but one of the pioneer physicians in embryo preservation for cancer survivors was right here in the city. If anyone could get me knocked up, it would be this guy.

Andrew and I met Dr. O. He was slight in stature, unassuming even, but his accomplishments in the field and accolades from colleagues were impressive. After reviewing my file he began to speak. "Well, your body has been through the ringer, but there is a lot happening in the world of fertility. Let's check you out." He inserted the probe. "Okay, there's your left ovary. And here's your right one. This one looks okay, not great, but okay. I see some follicles, which is good. I don't think your left one is going to help us much, but we'll see." While continuing to inspect my uterus, he asked, "What is your cycle right now?"

"It's every twenty-eight days like clockwork, and it lasts for three days."

"Okay, that's really good." He pulled out the speculum. After twenty-something vials of blood were drawn out of my arm, and some further discussion with Dr. O about my ovarian functioning, we went home. Andrew and I felt positive about the visit and left his office with hope. *Please help us.*

I was ready to be pumped full of hormones, IVF, suppositories, injections—whatever it took. A few days later, Dr. O asked us to come in. He started right out of the gate. "Your FSH is very high, but there's another level that will indicate if hormone injections would help us retrieve an egg. We're going to do that today." I stretched out my arm, and the needle went in yet again. We went about our lives for another three days. I could feel it. I could feel it so deeply. I was meant to be a mommy.

We met with Dr. O on Friday morning before heading out to the beach for July 4th weekend. "I'm so sorry. All your labs came back, and there's nothing we can do. You're going to have to consider alternative options," he informed us with compassion. Andrew grabbed my hand.

"Wait, what about those hormones that can overstimulate my ovaries so they pop out more eggs? What about that study in Sweden? What about… I'll do anything, Dr. O," I pleaded.

"I know you would." And then he was silent. I cried into my hands as Andrew came around and held my head to his chest.

"We can talk about your options whenever you're ready." I nodded. I'd spent so many years enduring FSH checks and annual sonograms, measuring my levels, and having conversations about baby-making, and it all came down to this moment. And it was over. I was in menopause. With broken hearts, we made our way to Dr. O's office door, one foot in front of the other. Andrew, with the humor that always rescues us, turned around and coyly asked, "So, Doc, I guess we can throw out those condoms we've been using for six years?"

"Yes. I think that's a fine idea."

Andrew and I went straight to the diner to see if French toast and bacon could fill the silence.

"Deb, it's okay. We're okay," he said, trying to reassure me that life would go on. But I didn't want to hear it.

"This is not *okay!*" I screamed. "This is so fucked up! We found each other, we fell in love, now we want to have a baby and we can't. I hate this. I hate my body. I hate the Hodgkin's for doing this. I hate it!" We held hands throughout breakfast as I pushed my food from side to side.

"Hey, let's go to a movie," he said.

"A movie?"

"Yeah, you love movies."

"I do love movies."

"So, let's go. We can walk to the theater on Broadway and see what's playing." I nodded.

We spent the weekend riding boogie boards in the water and running down the beach for a much-needed jolt in serotonin. It was good to get out of the city and feel the sand between my toes. We walked from jetty to jetty.

"We're going to be okay, Deb. Actually, we're going to be great." I smiled. *Just let him hold you up right now. Breathe.*

The summer rolled on. I saw clients during the week and spent my weekends at the beach enjoying my newlywed status. For the first time in our lives, Andrew and I made love without contraception. We weren't scared to get pregnant like we were in our early twenties, and we weren't trapped in the hope of conceiving a child every time we were together. It was freeing. *I guess that's a silver lining.*

Over Labor Day weekend, we took a road trip to New Hampshire with a bunch of friends, one of whom owned a beautiful summer camp on Lake Winnipesaukee. The seven-hour drive was unbelievably worth it, because when we got there we felt like campers again. We started the day in the mess hall eating Fruity Pebbles, frozen waffles, and Tang. Then, off we went to water ski, play volleyball, and climb/fall off the ropes course. The last night, while we were sitting around the campfire, each of us trying to make the perfect s'more, I realized it was September 2nd. *I should have gotten my period by now.* I usually got my period around the 28th of the month, and I was still pretty regular even though I was technically in menopause. I started sipping my Pinot Grigio a little slower. And then slower. *Could it be possible? No way, Deb, don't get carried away.* My sane brain was saying, *Deb, keep drinking your wine. You are not pregnant.* I'm not sure why, but I just couldn't listen to that. I put the glass down and made myself another s'more.

I shared my insane thoughts with Andrew as we drove the seven hours back to New York, and he agreed this was crazy thinking. But Monday night came and still no period. It seemed I was losing my cycle to menopause. I went to work. By Wednesday, I couldn't stand it anymore. I needed to address the flutters in my stomach. At lunchtime, I left my office, went across the street to Duane Reed and walked to the Clear Blue Easy aisle. I never thought I would get to experience this kind of excitement. I felt like a twelve-year-old girl shopping for her first training bra. I had dreamed of this day—maybe I had a baby growing inside me. Maybe I would be a mother. *Whew—deep breath.* I walked up to the counter and paid for the little stick. I got back to my office and went directly to the bathroom. After waiting three momentous minutes, I checked the little square box that was supposed to show a plus or minus. It was in between! Are you kidding me? I grabbed the box and read the directions again, slowly. It instructed me to take the second stick and place it in a cup of my pee, instead of holding it against the urine stream. But my pee was gone! I already went to the bathroom. I gathered my thoughts and my purse. I had two hours until my next client and I couldn't just sit there. I hailed a cab and headed home. I thought about calling Andrew but I couldn't—not yet. I had entered crazy town. I chugged two lemon-lime Gatorades in five minutes.

I walked in, threw my bag on the couch, and read the instructions again. For most accurate results, it said, "Collect a sample of your urine into a clean, dry container. Dip the absorbent tip in your collected urine sample for exactly twenty seconds." My heart was pounding, and I couldn't seem to control the joy welling up inside me. I opened the kitchen cabinet to grab a water glass. But then I saw the Waterford champagne glasses we got for our wedding peeking out from the top shelf. They were still in their original packaging. *If this isn't the time to break out the good stuff, when is?* I unwrapped a glass and headed to the bathroom. I was giddy. I was terrified. The white stick sat for three minutes in the beautiful crystal flute. I paced back and forth waiting for the clock to tick off its final minute. I couldn't believe what I saw: it was positive!!! Tears ran down my face. I called Andrew.

"Hello?"

"Hi, honey," I giggled.

"What's up?"

"I have news," I giggled again.

"What?" he questioned.

"I have news—big news," I said louder, almost screaming.

"No!"

"Yes!"

Now he was crying, too. He came home with flowers, chocolate, and a Cuisinart juicer. We were determined to do everything in our power to create a healthy environment for this little one, even if it meant a daily smoothie of kale, broccoli, apple, ginger, and lemon.

Once Dr. O confirmed my pregnancy the next morning, our first question was, obviously, "What happened?"

"Well, guys, our statistics are based on research. Whether it's a fifty-fifty chance, seventy-thirty, or one in a million. You were the money shot. You are the 1%. Maybe you should check out Vegas."

From the moment I laid eyes on the little circle thumping inside of me at my six-week sonogram, I was in awe. I knew my pregnancy might be complicated. My uterus could decide, at any point, that it was done with its job and just stop expanding. That would obviously be a very serious complication, but there was no way to know if it would happen. I treasured each moment and tried not to think too much. As weeks became months, a beautiful body with ten fingers and toes formed perfectly within me. I was speechless. The same body that had cheated and betrayed me was making amends and nurturing my most beloved gift. I couldn't have been more grateful. My belly continued to bulge, my hips continued to widen, and—I hate (but love) to say—the full-blown waddle commenced. Plenty of my friends had been pregnant over the years, so I had heard the play-by-play of morning sickness, sciatica, sore breasts, exhaustion, mood swings, back pain, and so on. People said that any woman who tells you she loves being pregnant is a damn straight *liar*. Yet there I was, feeling joy every day, and without pain or vomiting.

I allotted three weeks of preparatory shopping, gathering, and nesting prior to our baby's birth. I wanted to set up the nursery and give my body a break from walking to and from the subway every day. I was getting big. Very big. The countdown had begun. Friday April 18th was my last day of work. I was relieved. I just wanted to take a shower, rub cocoa butter on my belly, maybe apply some Good Morning Hope on my chubby fingertips and watch mindless television. Andrew was going out with his friends, and I had the apartment to myself. After a long shower, I put on my robe, prepared an extra large bowl of Cheerios with sliced banana and headed to my DVR. I was about to sit down on the bed when I felt moisture trickle down my leg. I had no idea what was going on down there. I could barely see below my belly button. I took off my damp robe and changed into blue and white leopard pajamas. I turned on the television. Minutes later, more trickling. I stood up and realized my pants were all wet. *Oh my God! Did my water just break?* I quickly tried to remember what we learned in childbirth class. I think they said it wasn't always the big-screen, dramatic rendition of water rushing out of your vagina like a dam breaking. Hadn't they compared my uterus to a balloon—instead of one big pop, couldn't it be like a needle prick letting out the fluid slow and easy? Before calling Andrew and interrupting his much needed boy's night, I called Kim, who was a labor and delivery nurse. After she stopped screaming, she instructed me to smell my underwear. *What do you want me to do?* She told me if it smells like pee, it's pee. But if it smells like bleach, it could be amniotic fluid, meaning that my water had broken. I took a whiff. It smelled like bleach. "Holy Crap!" I called Andrew and tried to get the words out—our baby was on its way! Within minutes, a panting Andrew burst through the door.

"Let's go! Let's go!"

"Why are you panting?" I asked.

"I just sprinted twelve blocks! Let's go!"

Matthew was born at 5:40 p.m. on April 19th, 2009. He was three weeks early, but technically full term. After hours of pushing, crying, ripping, and pooping, a nurse placed him in my arms and I lost it. My heart literally grew and wrapped itself around my six pound, two ounce miracle. "Hi, my love. I'm your mommy."

Hope has played a pivotal role in my life. She has lifted me from the bottom of the well and given me a floor to stand on. She allowed me to push through even when I was consumed with sadness. I'm not saying that hope can turn an orange into an apple; it can't. I'm not talking about magic, or even miracles. I think of hope as a best friend who laughs at your jokes, tells you you're pretty and smart, and helps create the sense of self only part of you believes in. It's all exaggerated and sometimes not even a hint true, but it doesn't matter. You can be anything—everything. Hope does that for me. She holds me up and says, "Anything is possible." I held onto hope and it paid off. Against all odds, I became a mom. My dream came true.

Chapter 16

Now I'm Starting to Get Pissed

FOR EIGHT WEEKS, WE marveled at Matthew. He cooed and we cooed back, he blinked and we blinked back. We must have looked like idiots to strangers on the street. We were so scared to hurt him in any way that we became a *little* overprotective. We held him like a Fabergé egg, always cupping his head and cradling him close. So when my friend Vicki, a remarkable mother of two, came over and picked him up out of his crib like a sack of flour, I cringed. Would she hurt him? Was it really okay to pick him up like that? *Calm down.* Every day we smiled from ear to ear in wonder and delight... until feeding time came.

I dreamed of being that mother who sat in the park, gracefully lifting up her shirt for her newborn to suckle with ease. That did not happen. Instead of my picture-perfect visual, I struggled and cried and felt inadequate in every way. Breastfeeding was hard. Matthew would latch for a few minutes, then begin to wail and pull away. Every three hours I would try again but the cycle continued. I called friends and lactation consultants.

The key suggestion was to persevere. Everyone said, "Keep going. It will get easier." So I did. Sleepless nights, sleepless days—misery and exhaustion. I didn't understand. Why wasn't this working? Needless to say, I was obsessed with my boobs. I held them, squeezed them, massaged them, and attached them to a pumping machine all day long to stimulate production.

One night, I contorted my nipple into yet another position so my infant could latch on, and I found a hard little lump on my right breast. I'm not sure how I knew. Call it women's intuition, clairvoyance, or just downright bad luck, but I knew—I had breast cancer. The other side of my brain, the practical part, tried screaming clogged milk duct, which was the more common culprit. After three days of massaging the small little lump with heated washcloths and soaking my body in warm tubs, the lump didn't budge.

Without sharing my palpable fear, I called Dr. M, the radiologist who performed my annual breast exams. "Come in today. We'll check it out. I'm sure it's nothing. Don't worry," she reassured me. I arrived not showered, with bags under my eyes, dressed in maternity leggings and one of Andrew's sweatshirts. Dr. M immediately took me to the back and felt the lump I had described over the phone. Her eyes reflected her usual calmness and warmth. I wanted to believe those eyes so desperately, and I clung to that alternative reality for the next few minutes. But when Dr. M rolled the sonogram machine over my right breast and honed in on my latest enemy, it was clear as day. This was no clogged milk duct. Her eyes met mine. I started to sweat. She inserted a needle. In that moment, my defenses kicked in and it was as if I split into two people. One who was hovering above and saying, "If this is the beginning of what I think is about to happen, I am not ready. I am not ready! I have an infant at home. I am a mother. I can't do this now." And then there was the patient lying on the exam table who didn't have a choice. Dr. M escorted me into the consultation room, a little 10 x 10 area adjacent to the exam room. At first glance, it appeared to be inviting, outfitted with beautiful chenille couches and warm lighting, but then the truth set in. It was the "you're fucked" room.

My mother and husband had already arrived. I called in the troops, and like true comrades they once again rallied by my side. We sat and waited. Then the white coats returned and they all had the look. I didn't need to hear the words. I didn't need to wait for the pathology report. Any chance that my hunch was mere paranoia flew out the window. This was real. I was about to enter the world of cancer once again. *Hold it together, Deb. Just hold on.* Dr. M reported the bad news with tears in her eyes. "This doesn't look good," she said. "We need to prepare for breast cancer." I truly cared for, respected, and trusted Dr. M. That probably made it a little easier than the first time around, when a team of physicians who I had just met bombarded me with news of Hodgkin's. Dr. M had been giving me clean bills of health for years and now there was a big letter "C" stamped on my chart, on my chest. The fear, fury, and desperation started to flood into my veins as it did when I was sixteen-years-old. It could have been the same day—the same exact feelings, the same exact fears. And then new feelings as well. Was I going to die? How much had it spread? What's the treatment? My hair was going to fall out, wasn't it? Would I be sick as a dog? How would I raise my child? The protective dam of confidence that I had spent a decade and a half rebuilding was swept away in an instant.

There was no getting around the pure and utter fear of breast cancer. Every year, I got my mammogram, MRI, and sonogram, yet here I was. Thrown for a fucking loop. My shock was complicated. I wasn't a cancer virgin. So even though I felt as if someone had just punched me in the face and fear consumed me, I knew what I had to do. Once you are attacked from behind, without warning, you are never the same. You may walk through life with a gentle saunter, but when the enemy reemerges—weeks, months or decades after battle—you brace yourself and spring into action. Even though I was devastated, I had to mobilize. I had the knowledge and experience needed to combat the upcoming weeks and months. I could see the future. For better or worse. This was big, and I knew it. So even though I was scared out of my goddamn mind, I also felt like I had years of self defense training. I was ready. Only time would tell who would win this round. *Please be me. Please be me.*

We went home after the diagnosis and I got into the shower. The hot water ran down my back and I cried. I cried so hard my knees became weak, and I found myself sitting on the bathtub floor. I wasn't scared of the possible mastectomy, and I wasn't scared of the chemo—both were awful, but also doable. I was paralyzed with fear—of dying. *Please, God, I love my baby.* A cancer diagnosis is a crapshoot. You hear, "You have the best doctors. Everything is going to be okay. You are strong." But the truth is this—no one knows what will happen. Every year I walked The Race For the Cure with friends and family and saw those pink memoriam names on the runner's backs. Those women, the women who were diagnosed, fought the best they could and died. They were just like me. For the first time in a long time, I felt alone. I gave myself the moment. My fragile psyche needed to be honored. If Dr. W had taught me anything, it was to let the process happen. But the moment was just that…a moment. I turned off the water and toweled dry. I couldn't survive the next few weeks, or months for that matter, with reality up close and personal. That kind of honesty would need to take a backseat while I tended to more pressing matters. If I survived, the time would come to reflect and mourn. Now it was time to fight.

I instinctively grabbed the nursing bra I had been wearing religiously for months and realized that part of my life was over. I threw it in the laundry basket and slipped on one of Andrew's soft oversized T-shirts. I was exhausted to a point I didn't think possible, and now, a cancer diagnosis. To say I was hanging on by a thread was an understatement.

Andrew knocked on the door. "Are you ready to make some phone calls?" he asked.

"Yep, ready as I'll ever be," I said. We'd been given names of breast surgeons, plastic surgeons, and oncologists. I didn't have much time to saunter around Manhattan and choose a doctor, but at the very least I needed a specialist who made me feel comfortable and safe (if that was even possible). The first appointment I could get was in two days. Two days! It seemed like an eternity, but I had no choice. Andrew and I did some research online and learned what the next few steps might look like. We read about lumpectomies, mastectomies, Tamoxifen, oncotypes and receptor status until our eyes blurred. I cried. He cried. It seemed like only yesterday that we were lying in each other's arms celebrating our pregnancy and now, this. Back and forth we went. From sobbing to spreadsheets, from screaming to appointment making—it was just how we got through those first few days. It was time for yet another Trapper Keeper.

It was 11:00 p.m. and I couldn't fall asleep. *What are these doctors going to recommend? Do I need a mastectomy? Do I need chemotherapy? In thirty minutes I need to feed Matthew, then I need to do laundry. I need to remember to call the second plastic surgeon to see if we can get an appointment this week. Oh, and I need to call Steph and Gigi to bring them up to speed.* My brain just wouldn't stop. *I have too much shit to do to feel overwhelmed.*

That night, a few hours post diagnosis, after I bound my breasts to stop my milk production, after I scheduled meetings with two breast surgeons, two plastic surgeons, and two oncologists, after I sang my infant to sleep with tears silently rolling down my face, I realized I was not the same person that I was at sixteen. I was not a newbie; I was a veteran. I knew this rodeo, inside and out, and I needed to get in the game. The doctors were using my previous chemotherapy, radiation, and surgeries to help them assess which road to pursue in my next treatment. My history was critical in creating the most effective medical protocol to cure the breast cancer invading my body. *Wait a minute. If the doctors are studying my history to help navigate through this mess, I should be doing the same thing. I can use my past, my scars, my memories to create my own personal survival guide.* The next several months would not only be an attack on my body, but on me—mother, wife, daughter, and woman. I wracked my brain and started writing a list of questions for myself. What had I learned sixteen years ago? What had I learned four years ago? What did I object to? What did I regret? What was I proud of? What did I fear? What mistakes could have been prevented? I wasn't going to be passive this time. I knew what I liked in a doctor. I knew how I wanted to be treated. I knew I wanted to be heard.

I knew how I personally coped with crisis and how I could guide my friends and family in their efforts to help me. It still didn't feel natural for me to ask for help, but I was going to do it anyway, because at the end of the day, it was important. I also knew what kind of patient I wanted to be. I would cross my own T's and dot my own I's. I wrote and wrote and wrote. I dredged up all my high-school memories, both pleasant and unpleasant. I recalled frightening scenarios and the coping strategies that were most effective. I stopped to consider anything that could help me get through this next chapter of my life. No matter how intimidated, how exhausted, how vulnerable, I would never again apologize for asking a question or requesting a sleeping pill. *Put me in coach, I'm ready to play.* And so began my battle with breast cancer.

Two days later I woke up for a marathon of appointments. Andrew and I sat at the breakfast table, poured milk into our cinnamon Cheerios, and laid out all of the materials we had collected. Scans, history reports, and lab results were all scattered before us. We discussed our plan of action while I pretended to be strong and confident. At some point, I teared up. "This is ridiculous," I said. "This is absolute bullshit."

Andrew nodded. The phone rang. It was the radiologist's office. My biopsy results came back and the cancer status was upgraded—very aggressive. Not mild or medium. *Fuck.* "Aggressive" means the cancer cells were multiplying fast and that it was imperative we begin treatment as soon as possible. I was ready to go. I was ready to get this crap out of me.

I had three parallel but very different goals mapped out. The first: destroy the cancer. Cut it out with scalpels, burn it with radiation, poison it with chemotherapy, all of the above—just kill the sucker. The next objective, which was ever so important because I was now a mother, was the adjustment to my new life without losing myself in the process. I would have to deal with the physical side effects of the treatments (baldness, nausea, mastectomy, etc.), maneuver through the medical system, empower myself as the patient, and maintain my voice on this journey. I vowed to honor my emotions. The third was about the world around me. For a long time, I couldn't differentiate receiving help from being helpless. But now, when everyone started to ask, "What can I do?" I planned to say, "Don't call, don't email, don't text—send *food*."

We met with two breast surgeons, one plastic surgeon, and an oncologist. Most of our questions were answered and we felt on top of things. All parties recommended the same protocol: bilateral mastectomy plus chemotherapy. Given my history and the probability that I developed breast cancer from the radiation I received as an adolescent, it was a real possibility that I could develop more malignant cells over time. The removal of both breasts was the safest option. Radiation, which is commonly used as a treatment post-mastectomy, was off the table. Human skin can only withstand certain levels of radiation in one lifetime, and I had already used up my allotment. So the game plan was definitely a double mastectomy. By the time the third doctor agreed with this regimen, reality set in that this was indeed happening.

My breasts were engorged with milk and drooped down towards my belly button. They contained the enemy and I wanted nothing to do with them. I didn't need to be convinced or counseled on the surgery. I was ready, willing, and able.

We decided on our team. Dr. C was the breast surgeon who would remove my boobies. Her body was petite, but she was a downright panther. From the first time we entered her office it was obvious she was as good as it gets—confident, smart, and quick. Her piercing blue eyes said, "I will get the sucker. This is what I do. No one messes with me." And I believed her. She wasn't warm and fuzzy. She was the kick-ass kind of doctor. I needed her to cut and cut well.

The breast surgeon's partner in crime is the plastic surgeon. Dr. B was pretty intimidating at first introduction. Head to toe, he looked like he should be propped up against a backdrop for a Vogue photo shoot. He was probably around my parents' age and proudly sported slicked back salt-and-pepper hair and thick-rimmed black glasses.

"My goal is to have you look in the mirror, in a bikini, my dear, a few years from now without it even crossing your mind that your breasts were constructed. They'll become part of you." I couldn't imagine that happening, but given his commitment and obvious proclivity for perfection, I was willing to place my money on him.

Dr. B explained that reconstruction plans varied from patient to patient. Mine would include three rounds of surgery. The first piggybacked onto the mastectomy, where tissue expanders would be placed in my breast pockets. He explained that a tissue expander is like an implant, but has the capacity to be filled over a period of time. A patient can start out with an A cup on Day 1, but as the weeks progress, saline is injected into the expanders and the pocket grows larger. This allows your skin to slowly adjust to its new size. The second, which would take place months later, was the exchange surgery where the expanders, having reached my desired cup size, were replaced with filler (i.e. silicone). The third procedure would be the nipple surgery. I was nervous but I really just wanted to get the show on the road. Concentrating on explaining the first surgery, Dr. B gave me the heads up that the first would be the hardest. Given that it would directly follow the mastectomy, it had the longest recovery time of the three. He then brought up the drains. "For at least a week post-op, you'll have six drains that will help release all the extra fluid from your body. After a week, we will remove them."

"So, I'm going to have tubes actually sticking out of me?" I asked.

"Yes."

"So just to be clear, these drains are plastic...and long...and they will be jutting out of me?"

"Yes," Dr. B repeated.

"How do they stay in?"

"Don't worry. They will not fall out. We suture them to you."

Suture? You mean staple them. To my skin. I couldn't wrap my brain around what these things were going to feel or look like, so I figured I would just have to find out when it happened.

Since my breasts were in full lactation mode, Dr. C had to schedule the surgery two weeks out. *I have to wait two weeks! That means two weeks of cancer multiplying inside me. Shit.* As she so eloquently stated, "We would like to avoid a bloodbath in the operating room, so we're going to wait for your milk to dry up." Apparently, when a woman is nursing, the breast's vascular system is filled with extra blood flow to aid milk production. I shuddered when she used the term "bloodbath," but at least I could trust her to be honest with me.

We came home feeling accomplished. I immediately researched remedies to help stop milk-making. *Bloodbath* sounded bad. After punching in some keywords, I easily found a well-reviewed method from a holistic website: "Place full cabbage leaves in a pot of boiling water. Once soft and translucent, drain and dry. Layer them on top of your breasts, removing excess water with a towel. Wrap tightly with a large ace bandage." It didn't sound horrible. I continued to read,

"The milk-drying process may be painful for some women." Just to be on the safe side and confirm that cooked cabbage wasn't some sort of cancer accelerant, I called Dr. C. It was safe. So, in the midst of preparing for the big surgery, I walked around the apartment smelling like a garbage dump, with layers of boiled cabbage wrapped tightly under a bandage, which was under an even tighter sports bra. I don't think it helped. It hurt.

The momentous morning began with the harshest of noises as the alarm siren blared at 4:45 a.m. I dragged my body to the bathroom, where I took out the super-strength anti-bacterial wash Dr. B had given me a few days prior. I read the instructions and repeated them aloud since my brain wasn't fully charged yet. "Wash your entire body once, the surgical area twice, and don't forget your hair." I scrubbed once, twice and then three times—why not? I felt my breasts and the hard lump that lay beneath. I didn't push too hard, afraid I would somehow puncture the tumor and send cancer cells spiraling throughout my body. *You are out of me today.* I realized, all too clearly, that I was also saying goodbye to my breasts. The same breasts that I prayed would grow when they were mere grape-size mounds at twelve years old. The same breasts that got the boys to help me with heavy groceries or a flat tire throughout my teens and twenties and—who am I kidding?—my thirties. The same breasts whose cleavage I revealed so proudly in my wedding dress only a few years ago. I exited the shower, dried off with a fresh-out-of-the-dryer towel, and threw on sweats, which had also been cleaned the night before. No germs. I checked the clock. *5:00 a.m. I'll give Andrew a few more minutes.* I took the time alone to go into Matthew's room. He lay there swaddled in his blanket. My mind raced and I let myself, for the first time since this whole thing started, feel the fear that was hovering above. *I'm your mommy and I will always be your mommy. I will fight with everything that I have. You are my most precious gift. I will love you forever— wherever I am.* Almost gasping for air, I picked him up and held him against my chest. *Breathe…inhale, exhale.*

"Babe, where are you?"

"I'm in Matthew's room. I'm coming." I wiped my tears with my sleeve. I put my baby back in his crib and closed the door. I had never in my life felt the kind of pain that I felt in that moment.

We were asked to arrive at the hospital at 6:00 a.m. We arrived at 5:45 a.m. No coffee, no water—just a stomach of nerves and knots. I reported to the 5th floor, where I was given a gown, robe, and slippers, and asked to wait in the adjacent room. After undressing, I was brought back to the waiting area, where my mother and Andrew sat. The nurse told me that this portion of the tour was part of pre-op, but I really didn't know what she meant besides putting on a surgical hairnet. Only a few minutes passed. The nurse called my name and escorted me into a room with a huge machine in the middle. *What the hell is that?*

"This machine is going to help us locate your sentinel node," she told me. "Just wait here, honey, and the doctor will be in shortly." *Sentinel node?* The doctors had thrown the term around a few times over the past two weeks, but it had always sounded like something technical that I didn't need to worry about.

A doctor sauntered in, and I immediately disliked him. I don't know what it was. Maybe the "I don't give a shit about you or anything else" air about him or his unshaven face that made me think he was pulling an all-nighter at the hospital or, even worse, the bar around the corner. Maybe it was that he didn't even introduce himself and I didn't know the name of the man that was staring at my breasts. But either way, this wasn't how I envisioned starting my day. And then it got worse. The doctor explained what he was about to do.

"You're having a bilateral mastectomy today with reconstruction."

"Yes," I replied.

"One of the biggest goals of this surgery is to ascertain whether the cancer cells have spread to your lymph system. In order to do that, I'm going to inject a low-activity radioactive substance in each breast that will make its way to your sentinel node, your first draining lymph node. Then, in the operating room, Dr. C is going to inject you with a blue dye that will be drawn towards the substance I'm injecting. She will then remove the sentinel nodes, and some of the surrounding area. This will help your team stage your breast cancer and determine an appropriate treatment protocol. The injection does sting a bit. Once it's complete, I will X-ray your chest to ensure that we have honed in on the node. Sound okay?"

Hell no!

"Yep, let's do this," I said.

Cancer usually spreads in a predictable order. Its first order of business would be to make its way to the closest draining lymph node. If the sentinel lymph node didn't contain cancer, it was unlikely that it had spread to other areas of my body.

"I'm really sorry you have to go through this on top of your really shitty day," the nameless doctor said. I didn't like this guy at first but he was growing on me. "Brace yourself, okay?" I balled up the sides of my hospital gown and clenched my fists. I closed my eyes and.... *Ouch!*

"I know. It really does hurt," he blurted. "Ready for the next one?"

"Yes."

Ouch!

After a few deep breaths, we walked down the hall together to see if the X-ray revealed the answer we were hoping for. It did. *Thank god.*

"Nice to meet you. I hope we never see each other again," he stated.

"Same here," I smiled.

My mother, Andrew, and I took the elevator down one floor to the OR's waiting room. When a nurse walked in and looked directly at me, I knew I was being called up to the batter's box. I'd been here before. Different disease, different statistics, but the same game. It doesn't matter how much I've practiced or how many home runs I've hit in the past. Each time at bat, when the curve ball comes barreling towards me, there is a new challenge. Hopefully, I'd hear that beautiful sound of the bat connecting with the ball...*crack*...and I'd start to run. But as we all know, it's anybody's game.

"Deborah Ebenstein?"

"That's me."

"How are you feeling?" Dr. C asked.

"Nervous," I responded.

"Makes sense. But don't you worry. We're going to take care of you in there."

The nurse came in and while preparing the gurney for transport, she blurted, "You need to take off your ring." *My wedding ring? Deep breath. No biggie. No biggie. It's just protocol.* I slid it off my finger and gave it to my mother. Lying flat on my back, I stared at my mom and Andrew's faces as the nurse pushed the mobile bed.

"Okay, we are about to enter the OR." My lips were curled in the shape of a smile. I was trying so hard to seem brave and strong, but my heart was breaking. Tears ran down my face.

Andrew's voice cracked. "I love you," he said.

"I love you guys. See you in a few hours." *Please, please, please, get me through this.*

While my family sat in the waiting room trying to stay sane, Dr. C began the surgery with focused energy, digging out every fragment of breast tissue that could possibly harbor cancer cells. She sent tissue samples to the pathology lab and prepped the now empty breast vessels for Dr. B. After three laborious hours, Dr. C placed her scalpel down and Dr. B entered the OR. I envisioned them giving each other a high five as they passed one another in the scrub room. Dr. B placed the tissue expanders inside my chest wall and connected them in all the right places. Once the expanders were set, Dr. B closed me up.

I woke up from the bilateral mastectomy in the recovery room. Recovery rooms suck. They are loud and confusing. You come to feeling like a Mack truck has hit you. I heard beeps, I felt cold, I needed to pee but couldn't, and my mouth was as dry as the desert. I needed ice chips. My eyes barely functioned.

And then I heard an angel's voice next to me: "It's okay, Deb. You just woke up from surgery. You are okay. My name is Kelly. I'm your nurse."

Bless this woman. She knew to come close to my face so I could hear her. She knew to talk slowly. She knew to repeat herself over and over since I would forget every twenty seconds what had happened and where I was while the anesthesia pulsed through me. I couldn't feel much, but I knew I was stiff. Tears ran down my cheeks. I was overwhelmed with relief. It was over. *Matthew.* I felt so lucky. I guess anytime you go under the knife there is always a fear that you'll never open your eyes again. And then when you do, you feel, well...grateful. My mom and Andrew were peering over me and I smiled inside. I picked up my hand and waved, because I was still too woozy to speak. Moments later, my stretcher was wheeled away and the faces of my family passed above me like a scene straight out of the movies. Someone was bringing me up to my room.

Once settled in the hospital bed, I started to focus. My first order of business was to check out the results of the past ten hours. What the hell was my chest going to look like? A war zone? Nipple-less mounds? No mounds at all? As I moved my chin down slowly, I held my breath. I smiled when I saw the pretty, nude bra with the small white flower in the center that I had purchased the day before. The doctor told me to come in with my own surgical bra so they could put it on me after the reconstruction to keep each breast in place while they healed. And my chest wasn't flat. It was more like I had the breasts of twelve-year-old Deb, like a large A or maybe even a size B. My tissue expanders were in, and they were already inflated a little bit, like a balloon that was twenty percent full. I know—it sounds a little weird and maybe a tad gross, but I was thankful to be the recipient of this modern technology. I'm not sure if I was smiling on the outside, but I sure was beaming on the inside. I hoped the cancer was out of my now-healthy body, and I even had some cute new boobies.

After I digested the miraculous success of the surgery and looked at my perky new ta-tas, I noticed them. *Drains.* Six long, skinny, clear plastic straws sticking out of my torso. Although I understood what Dr. B had said to me last week, I didn't really get it. A nurse came in to teach Andrew how to take care of them. First, she pinched the plastic tube and taught him how to suction the fluid down to the bottom in order to keep the tube clear of any blockages. *Ouch!* After performing this method on each of the six tubes, she detached each plastic bulb, measured its contents and emptied them. After reattaching each bulb, she sterilized the wound site and applied antibacterial ointment. The nurse kept a log of each tube's excretion that would help determine if the drains were working correctly. *What is that Deb juice accumulating in those plastic things attached to my hospital gown with safety pins? Gag!*

And then, suddenly, I felt pain. Let me say it again. P-A-I-N. I could barely move my arms, and my chest felt like a three hundred pound sumo wrestler was pressing a cast iron pan down on it. The nurse assured me that this was completely normal. I was instructed to keep my arms at my sides. I was not to raise them at all for two weeks in an effort to keep the implants in the exact same place the doctor intended them to be so that they would heal accordingly.

Andrew said, "Deb, you can press this red button. It's your morphine pump."

I pressed it. While I waited for the pain to subside, I turned towards Andrew and asked, "Babe, how did he sleep last night?"

"Fine."

"How is he doing with the formula? Did he take six ounces or four? Is he spitting up? Did your mom remember to give him a bath last night? Remember, I left his favorite blue blanket in the dryer because he spit up on it and I washed it yesterday. He doesn't like the yellow one. Tell your mom to get the blue one."

"Deb, he's fine. I promise."

I wanted to be home so badly—doing the things a mommy is supposed to be doing with her infant. But instead, I was here. I needed to kick the shit out of this disease so I could watch him get on the bus for his first day of kindergarten. *Deb, focus and listen to your doctors so you can watch him graduate college.* I needed to stop crying, get in the game, and start figuring out what we were going to do so Andrew and I could walk Matthew down the aisle one day. But first things first— how were we going to handle the next few months? We all agreed it was best for everyone if Andrew, Matthew and I moved into my in-laws' apartment, where help was just a shout away. It was going to take a village.

Two days finally passed and it was discharge day. To my surprise, I was conflicted about leaving the hospital. Although the sleep was not constant and the bathroom was shared, there was that little red button that made everything okay. I was dependent in every way, and found comfort knowing the nurses were around the corner if necessary. Once I was home, it would be up to my family and me. I was nervous. My loving husband spent two days sleeping on the window ledge because they couldn't find him a cot, so I definitely needed to get Andrew home before he ended up with a pinched nerve. And I was desperate to see my baby. But I was scared.

It was time to pack up. My heart wanted to race down the hallway to the elevator bank, but my body had a different plan. I walked through the hospital lobby with six drains hanging underneath my shirt, feeling pain with every step. Not to mention a hairdo that was obviously my husband's adorable attempt at a ponytail. I was sweaty and nauseous. *What if I can't do this? What if I just don't have anything left?* My mother pulled the car to the front, and Andrew basically did everything but levitate to get me into the passengers seat. I felt every bump on Lexington Avenue. I winced and gripped the door handle and thought about Matthew until we arrived.

Andrew opened the door to the apartment, and my mother hauled my bags inside. Matthew was lying on his play mat reaching for the stuffed clownfish dangling above him. My mother-in-law was preparing his bottle by the kitchen sink. I approached him slowly so he wouldn't be startled, but I really wanted to run full speed and jump on top of him. I leaned over his body, swallowing my pain, placed my head on his belly and inhaled his baby scent. Finally, I was home. He giggled. I kissed his toes, hair, cheeks, and belly button. I wanted to breathe

Matthew. A little while later, after a face-off between Matthew and fishy, nap time commenced. I watched him sleep for about ten minutes and then realized how disgusting I felt. Although I couldn't shower until the drains were removed, I washed my face as best as I could while keeping my elbows tightly to my side. I changed into cozy sweatpants and a pajama shirt and asked my mom to arrange the pillows on my bed. *Ahhh…*

It seemed like only a few minutes before Kim walked in. I knew she was coming over, as a friend as well as a nurse, to make sure we could manage this whole drain maintenance situation. Andrew was honestly the only person who could handle the job and even he was totally freaked out. *I mean, yuck.* After gentle kisses, Kim said, "Okay, let's see those puppies!" I lifted up my shirt and she didn't flinch.

"Andrew, show me what they taught you in the hospital." She was confident, solid as a rock, yet warm and gentle. Her calmness couldn't help but transfer to us (well, a little bit), and we sure as hell needed it. She watched Andrew suction each tube, measure its contents, and apply the necessary creams. She coached and validated him. She confirmed that we were doing everything right, and her presence reassured us. Andrew was an absolute trooper as I squirmed and cried. *Ugh. We have to do this three times a day for ten days! Just shoot me.*

After Matthew fell asleep for the night, Andrew and I lay down together in our bed. He turned his head toward mine. Our eyes locked.

"I love you," I said.

"Me, too," he said. "We're home. Now let's finally get a good night's sleep."

I unfastened the safety pins that connected the drains to my waistband and placed them next to me on top of a folded towel. I popped two Percocet and fell asleep.

With each day, the pain subsided. After ten days of sniffing and kissing Matthew, my plastic surgeon finally slid those nasty suckers out of me and I was free to cuddle, curled up next to him without much pain. The next several weeks were dedicated to physical therapy. Nurse after nurse relentlessly stated, "It's up to you how fast you heal. If you do the work, you will get better— faster." I was determined to regain my mobility so that I could prepare Matthew's bottles, lift him onto the changing table, and wash my own hair.

Andrew left to run some errands, my mother-in-law was in her bedroom folding laundry, and Matthew and I were in the living room. "Okay, gorgeous," I said. "Let's get this party started." I took out the Xerox copy of exercises that I received from the hospital and examined the first figurine. The goal was be to bring my arm straight up like I was a pencil. With my palm flat against the wall, I started to slowly slide my hand up. At 45 degrees, my arm stopped. I felt pain. A lot of pain. *Was I ever able to bring my arm all the way up there?*

"Okay, Matthew," I said. "Let's move to number two." He smiled at me as his baby swing rocked from side to side. I took the bar and placed it behind my back. Slowly, I lifted it up and down for ten repetitions. It wasn't that bad. Out of the ten exercises, I successfully completed five. The others were too painful, but I would try again tomorrow. Wiped out, I sat down next to Matthew's swing. He started to cry.

"Oh no, honey. No. It's okay." Realizing he was hungry, I got back up and walked into the kitchen to try to prepare his bottle. I couldn't open the refrigerator. I placed my feet firmly on the kitchen floor and used both arms to pry the large door open but it wouldn't budge. *I hate how helpless I am! I just want to feed my baby and I can't do it!* I was emotionally somewhere between mad and sad, enraged and defeated. I heard Andrew return from shopping and called for him. He saw my frustration.

"Honey, it's okay," he said.

"No, it's not," I said. "None of this is okay."

I threw myself a pity party until Matthew's bottle was ready. When he saw his formula, and the crying baby transformed into a smiling baby, my sadness lifted. *I'm here, and that's all that matters.* But I was still pissed. I continued to do my exercises twice a day and by two weeks post-op, I was able to raise my arms high above my head—like a pencil.

My body was now ready for the first of four enlargements. Each enlargement would slowly stretch my skin to prepare it for the next round of maximizing. I was both nervous and excited when I walked into Dr.

B's office. Marnie, the nurse, set me up on the table and said, "Deb, this is when the tissue expander does its job." She opened up the tight sports bra that had been a permanent fixture on my body since the surgery and examined the canvas. Then, she ran a small, round disc that acted like a stud finder across my breasts. "Ah, there they are," she said. She found the access points within the expanders and picked up a saline filled syringe. "Okay, here we go, honey. It's going to pinch a little." Pinch. *Ouch.* Pinch. *Ouch.* Then it was over. *That wasn't so bad.* Before throwing on my Van Halen T-shirt from their 1992 tour, I looked in the mirror. In seconds, I had gone from a small B to a mid sized B. *This is so weird.* I met Andrew in the waiting room and asked with a smile, "So, can you tell?"

"Yeah, hot stuff. I can tell." We giggled.

Three more enlargements to go before we reached the point of large enough, but I still needed to decide what "large enough" meant for me. Prior to pregnancy, and all of my adult life, I had been a full C cup. It suited my body, and I always felt comfortable with my size. However, there was something very intriguing about being in the driver's seat when it came to boobs. I never thought I'd be in this position, but now that I was, I figured I'd have some fun.

For the next several days, I stuffed my bra with all sorts of household items. First, I padded each breast with tissues, then paper towels, then socks. *So this is what it feels like to have porn star boobs.* Andrew thought I was crazy sauntering around the apartment. After disrobing I asked, "So, what do you think?"

"What do I think?" he asked. "Is that a trick question?"

"No! Really, what do you think I should do?"

"I think you're gorgeous, and I'm on board with whatever you want to do." A few seconds later, he added, "But I wouldn't protest if you decided to go for the double Ds."

"I knew it!" *I'm going to have to think about this one.*

Chapter 17

Four Rounds

SIX WEEKS AFTER MY double mastectomy, it was time. Chemo day, Round 1. I woke up, changed Matthew, fed him a bottle, and then heard Andrew yelling from across the apartment, "C'mon, babe. Time to go." I couldn't help but compare what was about to happen to my chemo experience sixteen years before. The medical professionals said that even though I might feel awful, it wouldn't be anywhere near as debilitating as the Hodgkin's treatment. As a teenager, I endured eight rounds. This time there'd be four. The only thing that would supposedly be worse was the hair loss. It would be immediate. No thinning, no time to think about it. Just gone. But at thirty-three, having experienced all my illnesses and childbirth, I had considerably more perspective about my body image. I wasn't going to emotionally plummet and drown in sorrow over a head of hair. But I was still allowed to hate it. I wouldn't pretend, to myself or anyone else for that matter, that chemo and all that comes with it was no big deal. If asked, "How are you doing today?" and the day was actually pretty damn hard, that's what I'd say. There was no room for anything but honesty. *Let the games begin.*

Dr. T was a slim, mild-mannered man with a warm soul, a funny laugh, and shiny shoes. He made the worst days a little easier because of his kindness. Mitch, his nurse, stood tall, probably 6'3", and always asked how I was. Both Dr. T and Mitch walked into the waiting room. Dr. T said, "Good morning. You ready?" Andrew and I followed them into the exam room. I was ready— and armed with tons of distraction materials. My tote bag held all of the essentials: two Gatorades, tons of magazines, a Ziploc bag of crackers, peppermint gum, and a DVD player. Mitch smacked my arm around to see which veins responded. I gave him a heads up that the juicy-looking one on my left arm was a trap. He winked and inserted the IV into my hand. "I'm going to start some pre-medications Deb. The first is Benadryl and will help with any possible allergic reactions. It's going to make you sleepy, so just relax." *Bring on the woozy.* I hooked up my earphones to the DVD player and started watching Season One of *NCIS.* Leroy Jethro Gibbs and I would be well underway in our murder investigation by the time the chemo started to drip into my body. Then maybe we would tackle a Navy kidnapping or hostage situation. Whatever the case, I'd be kicking ass in alternate reality.

During the next several hours Andrew read the newspaper as I dozed in and out. Every few pages, he popped his head up to check on me. Mitch walked in smiling, disconnected my arm from the IV pole, and said, "Okay, guys, see you next week for a blood count." We hailed a cab on 2nd Avenue and headed straight home to my in-laws. I walked in and kissed Matthew thirty times before dragging my body to bed. I pulled the covers over me and passed out.

When I awoke, I felt like I had the flu on top of a killer hangover. Imagine waking up from a night of debauchery, drinking Bourbon mixed with gin mixed with vodka topped off with peppermint schnapps. It was like some crazy flashback to my out-of-control college days. I'd been given an array of medications to combat chemo's side effects. I hobbled over to the nightstand, opened the drawer, and perused the drugs available to me. I saw the anti-nausea pills and the antacids and swung my arm like a lasso to collect the bottles. Down the hatch. *These will make me feel better.*

An hour passed, then two. No change. *If this is what I feel like* with *the meds, what the hell will I feel like without them?* My mother-in-law walked in and asked if I would like some cuddling company. My heart sank. All I wanted was to hold Matthew. Smell him, feed him, bathe him, giggle with him, and kiss his toes. I said yes because I couldn't say no. After a few minutes, I ran to the bathroom and threw my head over the toilet. Nothing came up, but my gut was in upheaval. I couldn't leave Matthew on the bed alone, so I grabbed his wriggling body and placed him on the bath mat. *I hate this. I'm so fucking angry. Deep breath. You can do this, Deb.* Matthew was smiling as his five-month-old fingers tried to grab my face. I smiled back and thought, *I love you, I love you, I love you.* A few days of back and forth to the bathroom and it was over.

I had three and a half weeks until my next treatment and my goal was to spend as much time with my little guy as possible. On a crisp fall afternoon, seven days after my first treatment, I piled four loads of clean laundry onto the bed surrounding my baby boy. He snuggled as I sang, "I'm a little teapot", and used my now completely mobile arms to create "here is my handle" and "here is my spout." He giggled when I tipped over. Between Matthew's poop, my hot flashes, his spit up, and my bloodstains, our laundry situation was comical. When Andrew got off his conference call, he joined us in the bedroom. He now worked predominantly from home. I folded the final burp cloth and Andrew grabbed my hand. "C'mon. Let's go. It's gorgeous out." We took a walk around Washington Square Park and watched a blues band jam under the arch. We looked like an average young family. People peeked into the stroller.

"How old?" a woman asked, smiling.

"Five months." Andrew wrapped his arm around my waist, stabilizing me while I pushed the stroller through the crowd.

A few days later, the inevitable happened. I woke up to find clumps of hair on my pillowcase. *Damn!* In high school, my hair thinned slowly. I never had that Mr. Clean look. This time, it was going to be hard and fast.

Clumps and more clumps showed up on the carpet and in the shower drain. So before I totally lost my fucking mind, I decided to take the situation by the balls.

"Andrew!" I yelled. "I want to shave it! What do I do?"

He ran down the stairs. "Really? Now?"

"Yes. Now!" I exclaimed.

I thought since he was a guy, he would have some knowledge of electric razors. I was wrong. We scoured the apartment and found one at the bottom of the linen closet that looked like it was from 1988. *Better than nothing.*

Andrew and I were both pretty punchy that afternoon. While Matthew lay on the floor playing with his music box, we embarked on our mission. We started by cutting off big chunks of hair so the razor would only need to buzz those closest to my head. The scissors enjoyed every squeeze. My hair fell to the floor and we cut with abandon. We'd completed half my head when we broke out the razor. Andrew turned it on. Buzz…

"Okay, you ready?" he asked with a devious smirk.

"Ready as I'll ever be," I blurted, squeezing my eyes shut.

He reached over my head, touched the razor to my scalp and… Ouch!

"Nope, nope, nope. Bad decision. Bad decision!" I don't know what we were thinking. I ran to the phone and called the closest Super Cuts. With a baseball cap covering the disaster underneath, I jumped in the car to have a professional finish the job.

"Hi, I just called to see if you could help me with… umm…my situation… Is someone free?"

"Sure, over here sweetie."

I took off my baseball cap.

"Don't ask. Just shave it all off please. I'm going through chemo." The woman was kind and asked if I wanted to keep a few millimeters. I agreed and she shaved off the hair that was betraying me for the second time in my life. I felt oddly empowered. I was getting ahead of the inevitable. I walked out looking like a cadet ready for basic training. One less thing to worry about. *Good decision, Deb.*

I arrived at my next chemo session with Andrew by my side and tote in hand. I knew which room to go into, which chair was mine, and Mitch knew which vein to use. We had a rhythm. *Maybe this is getting easier?* The IV bags slowly dripped into me and then we were done. This time around I planned for extra help with Matthew and allowed myself to sink to the bottom without worrying if I was going to forget his 3:00 a.m. feeding. Forty-eight hours passed and I felt good enough to join everyone for dinner in the dining room. I beamed from ear to ear when I saw Matthew's face light up. I sat between my boys. Everyone continued to talk about their day. I had nothing to say. I was well enough to get out of bed, but that was the extent of my strength. I sat silently, rubbing Matthew's arm.

After dinner, I climbed back into bed with my laptop. What was I looking for? I logged in to my email and scanned the unopened messages I had accumulated over the past week. I quickly browsed through them until something from my physical therapist caught my eye. The subject line read, "Give her a call." Last week, she had asked if I would be interested in speaking with one of her other patients, a young mother who was also going through breast cancer treatment. She wasn't sure if the other woman would be open to connecting, but she kindly passed on my information. I read the email. "Dear Deb, this is Emily's email address. She was very happy to hear that I had another client in a similar situation. She's awaiting your email. See you in a few days." I stared at the screen. *Is this silly? What do we have in common, besides this wretched disease? What if she just gave me her email address out of courtesy? Why am I so nervous?* I started to type.

"Hi, my name is Deb. I received your name from Sherri, our physical therapist. Thought maybe we could connect, given we're both going through this really shitty situation. I don't know about you, but I sit in my oncologist's waiting room every week between an eighty-five-year-old woman who tells me how beautiful I look bald and a sixty-year-old man who doesn't pick his head up from his golf magazine. I feel kind of alone as a thirty-four-year-old new mother with a baby at home. So, if you feel comfortable, shoot me an email. Best, Deb."

My heart was pounding. I basically asked a stranger if she wanted to be my friend. *This feels really weird.* Only a few minutes passed. I refreshed my screen and there it was—a response!

"Dear Deb, I'm so happy you decided to write tonight. It's been a shitty day, starting with a chemo morning, then Crayola markers all over the couch when my two-year-old couldn't find her coloring book and my husband telling me he wants to 'get busy' once the kids are asleep. *What?!*"

I laughed out loud. Andrew poked his head in to see if I was okay. I told him I was just checking email. She wrote:

"A little about me. I'm thirty-two. I live in Brooklyn with my husband and two kids—my daughter two, my son five months. I was diagnosed two months ago and have gone through four rounds of chemo. They call it the ACT cocktail. Is that what you're on, too? I have two rounds left and then I go under for my double mastectomy. What's your timeline? How are you doing? I would love to chat via email and hear some of your war stories, too. I don't tell most of my friends what's really going on because I just don't feel comfortable. It would be nice to have a cancer clique. Talk soon. Feel good. Emily."

I was thrilled. I couldn't write back fast enough. I told her she made me laugh. I gave her a brief synopsis of my medical past and the details of this latest chapter. Within an hour we wrote back and forth three times, bonding over sour stomachs but simultaneously craving every food possible, including the Huevos Rancheros I made Andrew order for dinner. I somehow felt like I was back in the world of the living.

After three and a half weeks of kissing my boys, doing load after load of laundry, eating raspberry ice pops, and swallowing tons of Pepcid, it was time for my third chemo session. Mitch asked, "So, how are you feeling?"

"Pretty shitty, actually. My stomach is in an uproar."

"Yeah, that's typical," Mitch nodded.

"My friend, who is also going through this, said the symptoms get progressively worse with each treatment. Is that true?"

"Yeah, that's true. The second is usually worse than the first. The third worse than the second and so on."

"Fabulous!" I said, rolling my eyes.

I pulled up my chemo sweatshirt that I'd ripped to my elbow eight weeks ago on the first go-around. It allowed the IV to sit comfortably while keeping my body snuggly and warm in the cold office. Mitch inserted the needle and we were on our way.

The first few days after that third treatment rocked me. I wanted to rip my stomach out of my body! I wallowed in bed, not knowing what to do. I was in pain but couldn't fix it. I was hungry but couldn't get up to make myself a sandwich. I was plummeting. Andrew knocked on the door and poked his head in. "You doing okay, babe?" he asked. "Are you hungry?" I cried. He was just as scared, worn out, and overwhelmed as I was. *Push, Deb, push.*

"I would love a peanut-butter-and-jelly sandwich, babe. That would be awesome."

"Coming right up."

Finally the worst of it passed. I was able to walk into the living room and lie on the floor with Andrew as we watched Matthew continue to battle his fish. We were both exhausted. Matthew started to cry. I looked at the clock and realized he was hungry.

"I'll make his bottle," I said. It felt so good to connect with my boys again. My body continued to fight me but I didn't care. I made my way into the kitchen, grabbed the formula, and warmed up my son's meal. It was normal and so powerful. I swallowed my tears and fed my child. That night, I looked in the mirror.

"Wow, babe, Mitch wasn't kidding when he said the treatments were going to feel cumulative. I look like shit."

"No, you don't. You look beautiful. You smell like shit though. Why don't you get in the shower stink pants—it's been five days."

I laughed.

Soon, I had my eye on the prize. One more round of chemo. The treatments were killing those nasty cancer cells, but they were wiping my body of its good stuff, too. I understood that this was a necessary part of the plan, but I was in fact gray. I looked the color gray, I felt gray, I saw gray in the eyes of my loved ones. Food even tasted gray, given that my stomach was a perpetual acidic volcano. I craved color, but couldn't remember what it looked it like. I needed a reminder.

Vicki told me about a program at one of the hospitals nearby. She described an event which sounded like a cancer patient's version of an ambush makeover—like the kind on Oprah. Its mission was to empower women by validating their insecurities about their changing bodies and softening the blow of the inevitable sickly look. At first I was skeptical. Did I want to be surrounded by women who felt just as crappy as I did? Did misery really enjoy company? But then I read the description on their website and saw that at the end of the event, I'd be given a goody bag of fun stuff from various manufacturers who donate their products. Free samples! I remembered how my classic mani-pedi sessions made me feel when I was at my lowest low. This kind of reminder could change the game inside my head. I clicked on the registration page and signed up. Then I emailed Emily.

She wrote back: "Tomorrow's the big day. I have to tell you—I can't wait to get these suckers out of me. So, what do the tissue expanders feel like? Is it weird? Have fun at the make-up session. Talk to you after this is all over. Best, Emily."

I wrote back: "Good luck tomorrow. You're going to wake up afterwards feeling pure relief. I'll be thinking about you. To your expander question: they don't hurt but they feel…well…uncomfortable sometimes. Like you're wearing a tight underwire bra—constantly. But eventually they come out and you get brand new boobs. I hope the next few days go quickly. Talk soon, Deb."

When I hailed a cab the next day to bring me uptown, my fear got the best of me. *Why am I doing*

this? I'll probably be the youngest person there. What if I run into someone I know? What if this just reminds me of how unattractive I look? Oh, screw it—just keep driving.
I chose a seat at the long, cafeteria-style table. On each placemat there was a make-up mirror surrounded by an array of beauty products. I read the backs of the creams, tonics, and foundations as other women started to trickle in. Some much older, some closer to my age. There were even patients wheeled down from their hospital rooms. We were all very different, and yet we felt exactly the same way. We needed a reminder of what femininity felt like.

A make-up artist introduced herself and started her speech on how well-being, health, and beauty are all interconnected. I was totally on board with the message. I just wished they were serving pink drinks with tiny umbrellas. She instructed us on the correct application of this and that and how to take care of our bodies during treatment, which apparently can wreak havoc on everything from your nails to your skin. Given that our immune systems were on the fritz, she emphasized cleanliness, sterilization, and the need to protect our fragile bodies from external germs. There was a lesson on how to tie a perfectly knotted scarf around your bald head if you chose not to wear a wig, and how to even out your changing skin tone with the right color base. Although my sixteen-year-old babysitter, Angie, taught me how to apply electric-blue eyeliner to my eleven-year-old eyes while she bobbed her head to Mellencamp's, "Cherry Bomb," this was a whole new bag of peanuts. I picked up a few tips, such as the best way to feather an eyebrow pencil to make it look like my fading brows were lush and natural, and scored some incredible palettes of lip gloss and shadow from Chanel and Bobbi Brown. The ice was broken over hues of fuchsia and lilac.

Then the women started to talk, some voices stronger than others. The fortyish woman beside me put down her lipstick and said, "Whew, I needed this. I just came back from my 113th CAT scan with that dye. Does anyone else get some weird reactions from that stuff?" Across the table, an eighty-year-old woman who had been wheeled down from her hospital room wiggled her silver eyebrows and said, "Oh, yes, darling. Hell, I look forward to my monthly CAT scan. It's the only action I get these days." I laughed out loud and recalled my embarrassment when I had to describe the very same sensation to the cute male technician so many years ago.

At first, it seemed a little silly to spend an hour talking about cleanser, toner, and eyebrow pencils when there were so many other pressing matters on the table. But then again, that was exactly the point. This was not a make-up lesson in Bloomingdales from a pushy saleswoman. It was a wake up call to reassure us that we were not crazy. We were all thinking the same thing—we wanted to live. Maybe if I looked better I'd feel better, and people on the street would stop giving me that second glance. Maybe feeling better has some sort of power. Maybe I'd live longer, better.

I've never been to an ashram, I hate yoga, and I find it difficult to meditate, but my life's crossroads have given me, well, insight. Everything is connected to a deeper meaning, which in turn creates a reaction inside me—whether happiness and fulfillment, or inferiority and sorrow. If something makes me feel good, how can it be bad? Lotion is soft, silky, and smells really good. Why not apply it to my temples? Eyebrows make my face look complete. Why not pencil them in? Adding some blush and bronzer to my gray face makes me feel human again. Why not apply it, even if my daily activity only consists of an excursion uptown to physical therapy? I guess, in a nutshell, we're all social beings who react to the world around us. Maybe when the day arrives that a man walking down the street stops to tell me how sexy I look with chemo skin and painted-on eyebrows, there won't be a need for this discussion. But until then, the message is clearly sent, by way of energy and awkward glances, that we patients are pitied. These superficial social norms tie us to a healthy world full of positivity and glory, which has been stripped from us slowly and deeply. And maybe, just maybe, that positivity will start to ripple and create a wave much more powerful than once thought.

With a freshly toned face and Chanel Bonbon glistening on my lips, I entered Dr. T's office for my last treatment. A part of me was expecting the staff to break out in song like I was living a Broadway musical, or for Mitch to pop out of a cake that said, "Chemo's done— let's have some fun!" But then the other part of me, the deeper, scared-shitless part, said to the five bulging clear bags hanging above me, "Make this count. Do your job, 'cause this is it. Your last shot. Kick the ever-loving crap out of those evil buggers. Please. Please. Please." And it was over. We hailed a taxi on Second Avenue, walked into the apartment, kissed Matthew, and I climbed into bed. Five days later I woke up and smiled. Chemo— check.

Chapter 18

Boobs and Broadway

AFTER I RECOVERED FROM my fourth and final chemo treatment, Andrew and I decided it was time for the next step. We were ready to move out of his parent's apartment and into our own. Andrew pushed the stroller as we followed a real estate broker up West End Avenue, across 92nd Street, down Broadway, across 88th Street, and up Riverside Drive. After seeing five apartments, Matthew was done. Nap time was fast approaching and we needed to make our way back to the village.

"So, what do you think?" Andrew asked.

"I kinda love the one on Riverside. It's small but feels good. And it's right by the playground."

"I agree."

Three weeks later, we moved into our first home. It was a beautiful building on the corner of Riverside and 92nd Street. Moving day was hectic, as most moving days are, but when Matthew jumped on one of the porcelain dogs in the lobby like he was riding a pony, the chaos turned to bliss. My first order of business was our little guy's room. It was a glorified closet with a window, but had great energy. I chose baby blue and chocolate brown as the color scheme and adorned the walls with pictures and decals. The rug just fit from wall to wall, and after the last stuffed animal was placed on the changing table, I collapsed on the floor. Andrew picked up Matthew, yelled, "Matthew sandwich!" and they climbed on top of me.

We had nothing on our calendar for weeks. No appointments, no surgeries, not even a blood count. Andrew went back to working from his office and Matthew and I were left to explore the Upper West Side. We strolled up and down Broadway, went in and out of clothing stores, picked up groceries at the market, and grabbed lunch together at the diner. It was time to start experimenting with solid foods, and we began our days with apple sauce or blended bananas. Then, green beans and butternut squash. Every day was a different discovery, whether it was a new jar of creamy something, a block we had yet to saunter, or a playground hiding new adventures. My stomach had returned to normal, and I was enjoying food right alongside my little one. *This is heaven.*

Before I knew it, it was time for my pre-op appointment with Dr. B. "Okay, let's see what we have here," he blurted out. The gown I had just slipped into was now on the chair. *Why do I even bother putting that thing on?* I stood in front of the full-length mirror and watched him examine each breast. After pushing, squeezing, observing, and squinting he said, "You look great, Deb. Let's talk about the exchange surgery. Like I've said before, it's much less complicated than the first. Your body has healed from the trauma of the mastectomy and has grown accustomed to the tissue expanders. I am going to open you up here." He pointed to the bottom crease of each breast. I felt lightheaded. Dr. B continued to talk and point. "And here is where I'll slip the tissue expander out and then replace it with the implant you choose." As soon as he said "slip" I began to see black spots.

"I think I need to sit down, Dr. B," I said.

"Of course, sit. Are you okay?" he asked with a worried tone.

"I'm fine. I just walked in here feeling so normal and now, well, I'm back again. I need a second."

With his seersucker suit, pink tie, and matching lapel pin, he was an imposing figure, but his voice was reassuring. "You're going to be okay," he said.

The only question left on the table was the filler. "Are you ready to look at your options and make your final decision on the implant?" he asked.

"Absolutely—let me get Andrew from the waiting room."

We walked in holding hands and sat on the beige velvet chairs meant for non-patients. Dr. B opened up a dark case and placed it on his exam table. It looked as if he was presenting us with a black velvet box holding a delicate string of rare pearls. Andrew and I nervously smiled at one another as we handled the first silicone disc, then the saline disc, then a large teardrop-shaped implant and finally a small round one. One was too mushy, one was too firm, one almost slipped out of my hands and landed on the floor, which I took as a bad sign. After playing hot potato for a while, Dr. B asked, "So, what do you think?" *I don't know! I'm picking out new boobs for god sake, not shopping for a sweater.*

I looked at Andrew. "What do you think, babe?"

Andrew looked at me and laughed. "I'm not saying anything."

I finally picked the gooey one. It called to me. Implants—check.

We went home and I prepared the apartment. I knew I wouldn't be able to lift my arms for two weeks, so I brought everything I might need from the upper shelves down to the counter—bottles, nipples, plates, bowls, glasses, stewed pears and peaches, and Cheerios. I created an extra-hands schedule, since I wouldn't be able to pick Matthew up out of his crib. Between my mom, Ina, and Andrew we had it covered. I bought all the medications needed for post-op as well as the bandages and ointment. I had it all figured out. Maybe I really could be in control? Hee hee.

A few days later, I experienced serious déjà vu. It was a cold December morning that began with a 4:45 a.m. wake up call. I had spent forty-five minutes the night before searching for the antibacterial wash Dr. B had given me before the mastectomy, and it was waiting for me in the shower. I read the instructions again: *wash your entire body once, the surgical area twice, and don't forget your hair.* Like last time, I scrubbed my body three times with the brown liquid that didn't lather and seemed to slip off my body. *I hope I'm doing this right.* After I was satisfied with my job, I grabbed the towel and ran to the bedroom to find my sweats. I packed my bag with magazines and extra socks. The buzzer rang from downstairs. I answered the intercom phone— "Come on up, Mommy." I waited in the hallway as the elevator door opened. "How are you doing, darling?" she asked with a large coffee cup clutched in her hand.

"Good. Ready. Time to wake up my big one." Andrew was already awake, brushing his teeth with one hand and trying to put on his jeans with the other. "It's okay—we're not late," I said, smiling.

"I know—I just want enough time to grab a taxi in case we have to walk up to Broadway at this hour."

"It's going to be fine." We both knew I wasn't talking about the cab.

I bundled up in a coat, hat, scarf, and boots, and then slowly opened Matthew's door. I took in his perfect face and couldn't believe how big he was. "Good morning, gorgeous," I whispered. "I have to go to my doctor, but I'll be back tonight. Safta is going to play with you this morning. And then Meema is coming later. You're going to have a great day full of Grandma love. I'll be back tonight to do our triple B routine" (bath, books, bedtime.) "I love you." *I'm going to be okay. I'm coming back to him in a few hours. There is no alternative. Don't even think about it, Deb. Walk to the door.* "Bye, Mommy," I said. "Meet you at the hospital."

"I love you darling," she yelled down the hall.

"I love you," I said. "Oh, and remember, he likes the pears and peaches now, not the apples."

This time was so different from the morning of the mastectomy. First off, there wasn't a cancerous tumor plaguing my body and soul. Second, I had formed a relationship with Dr. B and felt safe with him. I had grown accustomed to the paradox between his stern appearance and loose commentary. Third, this was a much less extensive procedure. Compared to a seven-hour surgery, this was easy breezy. I would be home later that day with a two-week recovery plan and only two drains for forty-eight hours.

Andrew and I arrived at the pre-op waiting area. The energy pulsing between us was obvious. "What did you bring to read?" I asked. "*The Times* and *The Wall Street Journal,*" he said.

"So you'll be engrossed while your beloved is being ripped open."

"Oh, and I ordered some adult entertainment to report to OR waiting room three for us 'friends and family' who'll otherwise want to jump off the top of the building by noon."

"That sounds about right," I said.

The nurse behind the desk called out, "Deborah Ebenstein?"

Dr. B held a thick blue marker in his manicured hand and began to design his morning masterpiece on each of my breasts. "Looks goods to me. What do you think?" he asked.

I don't know! I looked like a tic tac toe board! Dr. B called out into the air, "We're ready to go over here!" The nurse approached, stretched a medical hairnet over my beautiful one-inch crew cut, and pulled up the side rails.

Andrew was still at my side. "I love you babe," I said.

"I love you," he said.

"See you in a few hours with my new boobs."

The doors closed behind me and we made a sharp left into the operating room. *Hello again.* Three nurses were already prepping machines and talking in medical code. The fluorescent lights beamed; it was freezing.

"That juicy one right there in the crease isn't as wonderful as it looks," I informed the nurse closest to me. "It's a faker."

"Okay, it's going to pinch." *Ouch.* I winced. Then it was in.

"I'm going to give you something to relax you."

Great! Dr. B took my hand, told me everything would be fine. Then I was out. I woke up to a nurse hovering over me.

"You're in the recovery room, Deborah. Your exchange surgery went very well. Dr. B was just here and said you did great." *I'm so happy. I can't move, talk, or wiggle my toes. But I'm so happy.*

Before I knew it, my mom and Andrew were beside me. They reassured me that everything went smoothly and told me to rest. We had a few hours before I'd be discharged.

"How was Matthew, Mommy?"

"He's great, honey."

That's all I needed to hear. I closed my eyes and passed out. I awoke to the nurse again.

"I need you to eat something before you go home." *Home? Already? Give me whatever you've got and I'll eat it.* She handed me some crackers and juice. My body must have been working off a jolt of adrenaline because I drank the apple juice and swallowed the cracker in one motion.

"It's been several hours since your surgery," the nurse said. "If you can get dressed, you can go," she said. *I'm a little woozy...and nauseous, but I'm out of here.* With my arms at my sides, and drains dangling, Andrew helped me unwrap the hospital gown and gently slide on my clothes. Done.

"Hey, gorgeous!" I yelled as we walked into our apartment. Matthew crawled to my feet and giggled. *I'm home.* It must have been pure will that allowed me to swallow the food, get dressed, and walk to the car, because in an instant, I couldn't reach my bed fast enough. I was exhausted. My recovery wasn't that difficult, as I knew what to expect. No lifting my arms, no lying on my stomach, no showers until the drains were removed. Rest. Lots of rest. So that's what

I did. Within forty-eight hours the drains came out. I didn't even need to take Tylenol. I was shocked. Dr. B was right. This was much easier than the first go round. Don't get me wrong—it was totally annoying that I couldn't lift Matthew and needed another set of hands with me at all times. I was used to our alone time—and loved it. But I knew this was only going to last two weeks. I wore the surgical bra for fourteen straight days to make sure the silicone discs stayed exactly where they were supposed to while my body healed. And then the time came…

Andrew went out and Matthew was taking his morning nap. My heart raced as I walked into my bedroom and stood in front of the full-length mirror. I unbuttoned each clasp and removed the bra. There they were. My new breasts. Scarred, bruised, and evenly stitched, with some of the purple marker still intact. But they were beautiful. I pressed my fingers against them and felt their gushiness. They were so different than the expander, which felt hard and mechanical. These felt like me, instead of something inside me. I couldn't believe how perky they were. I sat on my bed and leaned back slowly, watching them. I eventually hit the bed, but couldn't take my eyes off of them. How many times had I wished my boobs would stay at attention when I was lying on my back, but they would inevitably collapse to the side? I couldn't believe it. They weren't moving! This was awesome! If I were going to catch a silver lining, this would be it. Dr. B was right. My new breasts were wonderful. And over time, I could imagine they'd make me feel sexy. And I'd never need to buy another bra! *Thank you, Dr. B.*

Chapter 19

Nipple Magic

A FEW WEEKS AFTER the exchange surgery, I reported to my oncologist's office for my three-month check-up. I had not seen Dr. T and Mitch since my last chemo session, and it seemed like forever. When my mom arrived, I was in my bathrobe, freshly showered and fully made up.

"You look beautiful, darling. You sure are getting done up for Dr. T," she commented while I slipped on my silver hoops. I was too nervous to admit that today was a big day in a string of big days to come over the next five years. It's a good sign when you are cancer-free for one year. It's great after two. Pretty freakin' fantastic after three. Amazing after four. And *hallelujah* after five. The three-month visits, which we hoped would turn into six-month visits, were difficult.

Andrew and I parked the car and held hands as we walked down Second Avenue. "You okay?" he asked. I shrugged. Fortunately, I was Dr. T's first appointment, and we weren't sitting in the waiting room long before Mitch came to retrieve us.

"Hi, guys. How's it going?" he said, bright-eyed.

"Things are good," I blurted out. "Exchange surgery is done and I'm digging my new rack.".

Unsure if he was supposed to look, or not look, remark, or not remark, Mitch sought Andrew's help and I giggled.

"Okay," he said. "Let's take some blood." I didn't need to tell Mitch about my veins—he was an expert. Dr. T walked in.

"Things look good, Deb," he said. "Your numbers are good. Let's get you on the table and check you out." He examined under my arms, pressing firmly and continually on each breast, my abdomen, and neck. He stopped for a second at my left underarm and pressed again. And again. *Breathe.* "Everything okay?" I asked.

"Yes, just feeling around. Everything is fine."

"Are you sure?" I asked.

Dr. T stopped feeling me up, took my hands and looked at me—not my body. I started to cry.

"You're okay. I don't feel anything. Deb, your odds are good. Really good. That's why you had the double mastectomy. That's why you endured four rounds of chemo. To give yourself the best shot of beating this." I had so much bottled inside me. I'd distracted myself by putting my life back together with Andrew and Matthew, decorating our apartment, and having the exchange surgery. But it was still there. It was always there.

You know better, Deb, a voice inside of me said. *This isn't over just because chemo is over. Your fear is real and valid. It's just part of the deal. But you're okay.*

A few days later, while we were singing "Wheels on the Bus" in Matthew's music class, my phone rang.

"Hi, Deb. It's Dr. B's office. We want to schedule your nipple surgery."

"Oh, okay—I'm kind of in the middle of something. Can I call you back?"

After finishing music class, I bundled Matthew up in his brown leather bomber jacket, buckled him into his stroller, and reached for my phone. "Hi honey, Dr. B. called and wants to schedule my nipple surgery. I don't know if I want to do it. I'm tired. I don't want any more surgeries. What do you think?" I asked.

"It's totally up to you," he said. "I will go along with whatever you want."

"I just want it to be over." We decided to talk about it later that night and I made my way up Broadway.

As I was walking with Matthew, trying to clear my head of everything except the moment we were in, I passed CVS. Before I knew it, I pushed the stroller through the automatic doors. I perused the colors on the wall and began to think about nipples. *What's so important about nipples anyway? Are they even attractive? They're kind of bumpy.* I didn't know. I thought about the beauty seminar I attended only a few months back. I remembered giving myself permission to feel pretty and the deeper meaning it served. *Maybe that's what this is, too? Of course I can live without nipples, but I want to move on. I want to feel good. I want to live my life to the fullest.* I picked up a polish called Color Me Coral, paid the cashier, and headed home.

I'd made my decision. That night, I told Andrew the day's details, ranked in order of importance: (1) Matthew pulled himself up on the rim of the couch and started to cruise for the first time! (2) Music class was a blast, and (3) Nipple surgery is scheduled for next Tuesday.

My two other breast surgeries were performed in the hospital, but Dr. B was going to work his nipple magic in his office.

When we arrived he went over the game plan. "Remember, this surgery is purely superficial. I will remove a piece of skin from below your belly button. It will take approximately thirty minutes to create the nipples, and then I will attach them. Even though this isn't general anesthesia, you will be totally out. Recovery is a cinch compared to what you've been through. This is it. Last one."

I stood at the elevator banks wearing a medical gown and turned to Andrew.

"Wow. I'm standing up, walking into the OR. This is so civilized." I took a deep breath. "I'll see you in an hour. I love you."

"I love you," he said. "Go get 'em."

The doors opened, and Dr. B's beautifully designed office, filled with custom seating areas and hand-painted wall coverings, had transformed into a fully equipped operating room. The bright lights, trays of instruments, leg warmers, IV poles, and machines clicking and beeping were all present. Dr. B and his anesthesiologist walked in and started the IV. *Here we go.* "Good night," I said with a smile.

After what seemed like a catnap, I awoke to thick bandages over each nipple and a line of stitches on my stomach from where Dr. B had gathered the necessary material. "It went really well. You look great. You can take off the bandages in seventy-two hours—no showers until then." I got dressed by myself, walked upstairs, no wheelchair or drains, and opened the door to the waiting room. Andrew looked up from his paper and immediately shot out of his seat. "You're done?" he asked, surprised.

"Yep—let's go!"

"I'll get the car," he said.

"That's okay. It's only a block away. I want to walk with you."

I was so happy that I had endured this final step of reconstruction. I slept off a good part of the first forty-eight hours, sweating out the narcotics. *I get to see them tomorrow. What will they look like? What did my nipples look like before?* I never posed nude or starred in a homemade sex video, so I didn't have documentation of my old nipples. Finally, seventy-two hours passed. During Matthew's morning nap, I slowly peeled off each strip of tape that held the bandages in place. I removed the thick mound of gauze. I was in awe. Although they looked like they'd recently survived a knife fight, I could see the authenticity beneath. They were bumpy and round, with rough edges, and the cutest little nipple in the middle. *You guys are adorable!* I covered my hands with anti-bacterial gel and touched them. It was strange since I didn't have sensation from the inside but my fingers could experience every centimeter. They were truly my cherries on top.

Chapter 20

I'll Take Boring Any Day

I'D BEEN DREAMING ABOUT this day for so long. My treatments were done. The surgeries were over. There wasn't anything left to do except live. And that's exactly what I did—in between my check-ups.

I chugged the mommy Kool-Aid and loved every minute of it. If it wasn't Gymboree, it was baby art class or swinging in the park. Matthew and I went everywhere together. He helped me pick out dinner choices with giggle communication. If he laughed when I said chicken, we had chicken. If he laughed when I said ravioli, we had pasta. It was just that simple. We lived day to day—for so many reasons. Everything had been so complicated for so many months, that I craved simplicity. And life with an infant brings you back to basics. It's part of the miracle. But even more significant, the main reason that I was determined to cherish every moment was that I had no idea what tomorrow would bring. If I spent my time thinking about the next doctor's appointment, fear and anxiety would rob me of the now. And my now was happy.

My one-year post-treatment anniversary arrived and, like all my other check-ups, I held on tight. *I don't have control over this. I have to hope. I have to breathe.* The day came and I passed all my tests. Andrew and I held hands in the back seat of the taxi.

That night, while Andrew was working at his desk, I picked up my laptop and started to write. My fingers typed whatever flowed through my head. "Do I really get to dream again? What if I take the plunge, dream big, and then, just when I'm the happiest I've ever been, everything is ripped from me? Will it crush me? Things are different. I'm not just a woman with personal plights. I am a mommy with hopes and visions for my baby boy. I want to give him everything. I'm scared."

Andrew looked up and said, "Okay, no more working. Computers off." I quickly closed out of Microsoft Word. It was better for him to think I was online searching for the perfect shag rug for our living room.

Six more months passed. I pushed Matthew on the swings, glued pasta shells to construction paper, and met other mommies in the neighborhood for play dates. My life seemed, well, normal. With every night that I tucked Matthew into his crib and then slipped into bed with Andrew, I stepped a little further into this reality. Maybe this was my life now? Maybe I would get to live happily ever after? Maybe…

I passed my eighteen-month anniversary with flying colors. The door to our future opened a little further. "Andrew, I want to look at houses—outside of the city. What do you think?"

He smiled. He understood what a big step it was for me to believe in a tomorrow. "Where do you want to go?" he asked.

"Well, I know you're not going to move to New Jersey."

"Correct," he smirked. *Silly boy*. He'd never get it. We decided to check out Westchester.

I grew up riding my bike to the park, chasing after the ice cream truck, and trick-or-treating up and down the block. I wanted that for Matthew. We had a punch list of criteria when we researched towns in Westchester County. Andrew needed an easy commute to work, and we wanted enough space for guests and a backyard that could handle a swing set and a barbeque. As the real estate broker drove us around several towns, showing us charming colonials and contemporary homes, we took in the scenery. The streets were lined with trees in full bloom. Kids played soccer on manicured front lawns. We loved the natural beauty of the area, but none of the houses felt right. *Maybe this isn't for us? Should we stay in the city?* And then our broker showed us his last listing. It was a beautiful 1930s English Tudor with an original stone fireplace and oak floors. We pulled into the circular driveway and I studied the trim detail and stone patio. As we approached the front door, I was sent back in time.

"I *love* that smell," I exclaimed. "Is that honeysuckle?"

"Yes!" Andrew said with just as much enthusiasm. "There it is…right there!"

You think you know everything about a man, and then he says, "I *love* honeysuckles, too," and you fall in love all over again. I took three steps into the house. *This is it.*

We closed on Labor Day Weekend and drove straight to our new home. As we pulled into the driveway, tears of joy fell down my face. *Is this really happening?* My mother and a two-and-a-half-year-old Matthew were already kicking a ball in our new front yard. I opened the car door and heard, "Mommy!" Matthew ran towards me and jumped into my arms. "Are you ready to see our new house baby?" "Yes, yes, yes!" Andrew opened the door and then swept me off the ground and carried me, bridal style, over the threshold. Matthew didn't know where to run first. The house was massive compared to our tiny apartment. A few minutes later, the moving trucks arrived. *We're home.*

My history has taught me so much—the good, the bad, the terrifying. It granted me the ability to revel in the glory of being a suburban housewife. Nothing makes me happier than driving my toddler to preschool, giving a friendly honk on Main Street, burning meatballs on the stovetop, and even hauling our garbage cans to the curb. I am so overwhelmingly grateful for simplicity. The bottom line—I'll take boring any day.

Epilogue

Iᴛ's ᴀ ʙᴇᴀᴜᴛɪғᴜʟ ꜱᴜᴍᴍᴇʀ day—blue skies, soft breeze and the perfect amount of shade covers our backyard by four o'clock. I set my computer down on the patio table and think about how I should end this memoir. Andrew is marinating shrimp and prepping burgers for the barbeque. Matthew, now five years old, is pretending his swing set is a submarine. He turns his steering wheel vehemently through imaginary rough waters. Our latest miracle, three week old Chloe, is curled up in my arms. Can this be real? Am I really this lucky? Some may not consider my life "lucky" per se, but I can't think of a better word to describe how I feel in this moment.

Chloe falls asleep and I transfer her into the bassinet. I return to the patio table, sit down and begin to stroke my Hodgkin's scar. The slow, clockwise motion takes me back in time. Although the scar has faded, its message continues to guide me. My road to recovery went far beyond my final treatment. I lost myself to Hodgkin's, but when I broke out of the darkness, having mourned a lost girl, I reemerged an empowered young woman.

Our family starts to arrive. Andrew finishes his barbeque masterpiece. Parents, nieces and nephews, brothers and sisters grab paper plates and start to dig in. "You nailed it honey. This is delicious." He winks at me. As ketchup and mustard fly around the table, I take a moment to honor my second scar. I recall the sixty-two days of ITP—the debacle that propelled me to find my voice.

"Mommy, what's the treat tonight?" Matthew shouts across the table. "How about ice cream sundaes?" The kids all squeal delight. My heart is full. People get up from their seats and start cleaning up. The kids run back to the swing set, hoping to spot a great white shark through the periscope. As I clear the table and offer to refill empty wine glasses, I look down and admire how my blouse rests perfectly over my braless chest. I exhale. That's what you call a silver lining. My scars from breast cancer, physical and beyond, are fresher than the others but seem to be healing. They are the scars of a veteran. A woman who learned to empower herself in every way possible.

I place the pints of chocolate, mint chocolate chip, and mango sorbet in the middle of the table. Matthew comes running to help and grabs the toppings tray—M&Ms, rainbow sprinkles, gummy bears, whipped cream and hot fudge. He yells, "treat time!" and the chairs are filled again. We end a delicious meal with decadence and laughter.

Our family says goodnight and I finish up in the kitchen. My mother wraps her arms around me for an extra long hug even though I'll be seeing her again in forty-eight hours. I go upstairs to find Matthew, Andrew, and Chloe reading bedtime stories. I crawl under the covers to join them, and like every night, I linger for an extra few minutes to watch Matthew fall asleep. I tip toe out of his room and find myself standing in the hallway. I slide my back down the wall and sit crisscross apple sauce on the floor. I look to my right where Matthew peacefully sleeps entwined with his two favorite bears. I turn left and watch Chloe through the slats in her crib. She is drifting off to sleep while fascinated by the pink elephant dangling above. This is my favorite place in the entire world.

I walk into our bedroom and Andrew has placed my computer on our bed, knowing I must complete my work tonight. I log in and start to type. "Did you figure out how you are going to end the book?" he asked. I reply, "I think so."